THE
TRUE HAPPINESS
WORKBOOK

Abha Sharma is an author and personal development coach from India. *The True Happiness Workbook* is her sixth book, a culmination of years of searching for answers to the secrets of existence. Her earlier books include *Vediquant: Vedantic Truth in Quantum Science* (2023), *The Night of Fear* (2020) and three books in *The Making of the Greatest* series, all published by Rupa Publications. She believes in the democracy of knowledge, and that there should be no barriers to learning and sharing that knowledge. She has a master's degree in English literature and is a qualified university-level educator, having worked with international industry leaders and higher education institutions as an English language educator. Her work and life are driven by the quest to unravel the mysteries of life, to help people discover harmony within themselves. You can connect with her on her website or on LinkedIn:

https://authorabhasharma.com/
https://www.linkedin.com/in/abha-sharma-a1774a169/

Also by the author:

Vediquant: Vedantic Truth in Quantum Science
The Night of Fear
The Making of the Greatest: Mark Zuckerberg
The Making of the Greatest: Warren Buffett
The Making of the Greatest: Jack Ma

THE TRUE HAPPINESS WORKBOOK

A Step-by-Step Journey to Bliss

ABHA SHARMA

Published by
Rupa Publications India Pvt. Ltd 2025
161-B/4, Gulmohar House,
Yusuf Sarai Community Centre,
New Delhi 110049

Sales centres:
Bengaluru Chennai
Hyderabad Kolkata Mumbai

Copyright © Abha Sharma 2025

The views and opinions expressed in this book are the author's own and the facts are as reported by her; these have been verified to the extent possible, and the publishers are not in any way liable for the same.

All rights reserved.

No part of this publication may be reproduced, transmitted, or stored in a retrieval system, in any form or by any means, electronic, mechanical, photocopying, recording or otherwise, without the prior permission of the publisher.

P-ISBN: 978-93-7003-615-4
E-ISBN: 978-93-7003-178-4

First impression 2025

10 9 8 7 6 5 4 3 2 1

The moral right of the author has been asserted.

Printed in India

This book is sold subject to the condition that it shall not, by way of trade or otherwise, be lent, resold, hired out, or otherwise circulated, without the publisher's prior consent, in any form of binding or cover other than that in which it is published.

Contents

Preface   *vii*

1. Why Most Self-Help Books Do Not Help   1
2. Let's Face It   11
3. Pain Is Real   18
4. Separate the Pain from the Suffering   24
5. You Are Not Your Pain   36
6. What Are You?   45
7. The Path to Finding the Answers   53
8. The Method and the Route   68
9. You Are Not the Body   89
10. You Are Not the Mind   102
11. The Subtle Body   117
12. You Are the Witness   128
13. The Mystery of the Witness   139
14. The Enigma Called Maya   151
15. The Realization—the End of All Suffering   167

16. A Danger and A Warning	176
17. The 'How' Question	186
18. Conclusion	194
Acknowledgements	198
Notes	200
Suggested Reading	208
Bibliography	210

Preface

In the constant flux of life, once in a while, our otherwise tireless mind pauses, and asks us where we are going. In such moments, we try to make sense of what we have surrounded ourselves with, knowingly or unknowingly. Such pauses allow the whispers of the cosmos to gently drop hints of the blissful revelation that lies behind a thin veil of ignorance. Yet, for most of our lives, we look away, pretending to not hear the whispers, lying to ourselves, till pain and suffering surreptitiously creep up on us.

If understood correctly, these difficult times are opportunities, windows to finding a permanent solution to unhappiness. Instead, we grapple with suffering, often attempting to combat it with animosity, an endeavour destined to fail. We hate suffering, we judge it, and we run away from it. We refuse to see that suffering is to be understood, not despised. But, if the realization dawns on us that there is something beyond the apparent, and we start paying attention to the whispers, we will begin to hear the notes of the grand symphony of the cosmos. That which we seek is within us; we just do not recognize it, as William Shakespeare observed:

> Such harmony is in immortal souls;
> But whilst this muddy vesture of decay
> Doth grossly close it in, we cannot hear it.[1]

We may not acknowledge it, but all of us are affected by the mysteries of existence, by what physicist Brian Greene calls 'the rich duality of life and death'.[2] Deep inside, we know that there is a universal truth hidden somewhere, but we do not think it is worth our while to explore it. Instead, we spend our lives chasing superficial goals—acquiring surface polish through money, popularity, relationships and possessions, and most insidiously, by nourishing our egos.

Then one day, the reality of death confronts us, either at the end of our own lives, or on the loss of a loved one, or in times of great suffering. We realize that our constant striving to acquire the surface polish is meaningless, rendered insignificant by the passage of time, like the vivid imagery in P.B. Shelley's 'Ozymandias':

> Nothing beside remains. Round the decay
> Of that colossal Wreck, boundless and bare
> The lone and level sands stretch far away.[3]

In such troubled times, we seek answers. Ironically, we demand answers from life, yet we never pay attention to the subtle hints that life scatters across our path. Life, too, is no meek player. It waits for us to find the solutions ourselves. That is the beginning of our quest.

To find the answers to life's mysteries has been a grand project in every age, through a variety of means including science, philosophy, religion and psychology. The roads are many, but the destination remains the same. There is no perfect path; all you need to do is to seek the truth through the path that appeals to you.

My book *Vediquant: Vedantic Truth in Quantum Science* (2023) explores the quest for the truth of our existence through two widely different approaches—Vedanta and quantum science, and is for those who want to explore the path of deep science and spirituality together. The profound aspects of Vedantic philosophy are increasingly being echoed in the contemporary findings of quantum physics. The parallels between the two disciplines are awe-inspiring. The most mysterious aspects of our existence are reflected in quantum science too, and *Vediquant* is an in-depth exposition and exploration of just that.

The aim of the book in your hands too is to help you arrive at the truth of our existence, but this journey takes into account pain and suffering—a peculiar road towards realizing the truth. You may exit from this journey any time you want, but herein lies the catch. If you escape from studying your suffering, you will never be free from it. But if you utilize your suffering to understand the deeper truth, which is the destination of this road, you will find lasting happiness.

Vedantic enquiry, especially through Advaita Vedanta, the approach adopted in this book, is one among numerous ways of arriving at the Ultimate Truth. We can search for the deepest secrets of the cosmos in outer space or right here, in our own minds. For some, religion might be the answer. For others, science may seem more satisfying. Then there are those who might want to adopt the path of personal experiential learning, and yet others would want to explore the human mind. Vedanta is the path that needs only contemplation, and this workbook is designed to help you with that. Let us calm our minds and attune ourselves to the blissful symphony of the cosmos. Welcome to the journey towards peace and bliss!

1

WHY MOST SELF-HELP BOOKS DO NOT HELP

'Whoso wears the form, must wear the chain,'[1] wrote Swami Vivekananda in *The Song of The Sannyasin* (1895)—a profound exposition of the reality of our existence encompassing the range of our experiences, from the mundane to the exalted. Pain and suffering are inseparable parts of life. Anyone who bears the form of a living being will have to experience pain and suffering. That is inevitable. However, like a glimmer of hope in the dark, in the same poem, Vivekananda adds, 'Thine only is the hand that holds the rope that drags thee on.' When we suffer, we fail to acknowledge one fundamental truth—the power to free ourselves from suffering lies within us. While this idea is empowering, it can also be overwhelming, because we may not know where to begin. We all suffer, but we are unaware of how to find release from our suffering.

Through the centuries, humankind has sought answers to this existential dilemma. Humans have explored, learnt and experimented with various ways of dealing with suffering. From psychiatry to religion, from science to art, from psychology to philosophy, the human mind has constantly striven to find answers. Every approach has made its unique and valuable contribution to our understanding of the human condition.

Each approach provides a treasure trove of possible solutions. Therefore, instead of trying to establish the superiority of one over the other, it would be more fruitful to adopt the approach that appeals to you. Not all minds think alike. Therefore, each person will find solace in the approach that appeals most to their mind. The destination, as mentioned earlier, remains the same—understanding why things happen as they do in this world, so that we can find answers to our suffering and release from it.

If you are inclined towards religion, you are likely to find ready answers to your questions. If you are spiritual, you will seek a direct revelation, beyond the ready answers that are given to you. If you are looking for logical explanations to your problems, science will appeal to you. If you want to reconcile logic with subjectivity, psychology will feel more convincing to you. In the words of Y. Keshava Menon, 'The philosopher begins where the scientist leaves off, and the sage knows that what they both express are aspects of a unity, which he knows without the intervention of observation or inference.'[2]

You may find solutions to your suffering through a single approach, or in a combination of approaches. The important thing is to take the first step—recognize that you need help and seek it. One way of seeking answers to our problems is through readily available self-help content, especially books.

WHY MOST SELF-HELP BOOKS DO NOT HELP

In times of trouble, you might pick up a self-help book, hoping to find a way out of your suffering. But how effective are even the most popular self-help books?

Often, we come across people who remark that they felt a sudden inspirational high after reading a self-help book, but had no idea how to apply its ideas in their own life to ease their pain. The motivation and solace last as long as you read the book, but as soon as you finish it, you go back to being miserable.

In the experience of ordinary people like us, including this author's experience as a life coach working with people in distress, most available self-help books present generic observations and do not address your individual problem. Every person's pain is unique; there cannot be a blanket solution for everyone's problems.

At times, self-help books provide cosmetic solutions. If there is a thorn in your flesh, you cannot get rid of the pain by breaking off the top of the thorn, or by prodding it, or by applying a painkiller to the affected area. The pain can only be cured by removing the *entire* thorn. However, instead of helping you do that, some self-help books focus on the importance of positive thinking. But when you are in pain, no amount of positive thinking can help you take your mind off the pain.

Moreover, you are blamed for your own suffering. Some self-help content suggests that somehow you are the cause of your own problems—you either think wrongly, or you respond wrongly, or you have negative thought patterns. The claims often turn into a shame-game. You end up *feeling bad about feeling bad.* No amount of affirmation or wishing for manifestation can help you, if deep inside, you are constantly blaming yourself.

Often, such books set a guilt-trap wherein you wonder why an idea that worked for A or B is not working for you.

However, the most important reason why self-help books are often inadequate is that while they are full of promissory talk about useful concepts, they do not indicate how to use or apply such concepts. Like window shopping, you can see the goods from a distance and imagine that they might be useful, but unless you buy them and use them, you will never know whether or not these *will* make a difference to your life.

> The following are real-life examples from my life-coaching sessions. Names and environments have been changed to protect identities.
>
> - Twenty-eight-year-old management professional Arpit had been facing stress because of his workplace environment. On a friend's suggestion, he started listening to motivational audiobooks at the start of each day. For the first few days, he felt a boost of energy and was inspired to look at the positive side of things. But soon, he found himself confused about how to apply those ideas to his own situation. The inability to find solutions to his problems quickly turned into frustration. A few days later, Arpit starting blaming himself for not being 'intelligent' enough to manage his own mind. Instead of getting diminished, his misery increased.

- Misha, a student preparing for the gruelling all-India engineering entrance exam, had been experiencing anxiety and having depressing thoughts for some time. After over a year of intense preparation, and with only a few more months left until the exam, she started experiencing symptoms of burnout. Her alarmed parents got her a couple of motivational books, which she eagerly read. However, reading those books had a strange outcome. An otherwise confident person, Misha developed self-doubt. She understood the ideas in the books, repeated the inspirational quotes mechanically, tried affirmations, but found herself incapable of applying them to her own situation. That led her to believe that she was somehow a failure, a belief she extended to her preparation for the entrance exam too. Again, instead of Misha feeling more reassured, the final outcome was an increase in her distress.

We all come across motivational content on social media too. How many of those ideas actually help us?

The lure of Eastern spiritual traditions has often inspired celebrities and ordinary people alike, particularly from the West, to pack their bags and come to India. Among the Western celebrities who came to India in search of spiritual answers were the British rock band The Beatles, Apple co-founder Steve Jobs and Facebook co-founder Mark Zuckerberg. These people carried back some inspiration, but did these trips really help them find lasting solutions to life's challenges? When we are seeking answers to the deepest of life's mysteries, superficial efforts like seeking inspiration in people or places or following popular trends seldom help. They might provide some help, but they cannot give you deep, enduring solutions.

HOW THIS BOOK IS DIFFERENT

This book goes beyond mere motivation. It aims to lead you to the root of your problems, to help you come out of them through easy, practical methods that you can apply as you go through the routine of your daily life. This book does not just talk to you; it listens to you and handholds you out of your misery. That is why it has been designed as a special workbook. The exercises that start from the end of Chapter 3 help you discover yourself, bit by bit, till you understand who and what you truly are. Instead of providing generalized solutions, it helps you apply the ideas to your unique situation.

The exercises will reveal to you layers of your own personality, the reality of your body, mind and soul. Once you get a glimpse of that, you will have a unique solution to your suffering. Since we all evolve throughout our lives, you can come back to this workbook and go through the exercises again, as many times as you want, so that you can figure out why something is troubling you. Hence, this workbook is not meant for a one-time read; it can be your companion for life. As and when difficulties arise in your life, you will find practical help in these pages.

This workbook draws upon a powerful system of thought that is ancient, yet timeless, and that has the extraordinary advantage of having provided humankind with profound answers to suffering through millennia. Due to its deep insights into the complexities of human existence, it transcends time, space, culture and personal inclinations. This incredible storehouse of knowledge is known as Vedanta.

Vedanta is the essence of the Upanishads—Vedic texts that deal with the most fundamental questions of existence. However, the teachings of Vedanta have never been more relevant than in contemporary times because these constitute an incredible meeting ground of seemingly divergent approaches. While being a logic-based system of thought, Vedanta also values pure faith. It enquires into the subtle nature of existence, but also takes into account the physical presentations of reality. Speaking to you of the highest truths, it also asks you to examine your everyday experiences. It does not ask you to place blind faith in what the scriptures or sages say. It only helps you understand your own condition, and thereon arrive at solutions to your suffering. In this book, the term Vedanta will refer primarily to Advaita Vedanta, the school of non-dualism.

The relevance of Vedantic philosophy is increasingly being recognized across the world. Contemporary developments in quantum science have led to a paradigm shift in our understanding of the functioning of the Universe, with striking parallels emerging between modern science and this ancient philosophy (see the 'Suggested Reading' section). What came first is unimportant. What is crucial to acknowledge is how, time and again, different systems of thought and disciplines point to the same truth.

Hence, this workbook draws upon the practical approach of Vedantic enquiry, which is similar to the scientific approach, since it takes you to the root of the problem rather than trying to cure the symptoms. Vedanta is that system of knowledge that teaches you how to cut loose the rope that binds you to your sorrows. With a deeper understanding of its approach, this workbook can guide you to the steady evolution of your soul.

THE METHOD OF THIS WORKBOOK

Since the goal is seemingly difficult, the workbook follows a process that makes it easier for you to reach it. It is like climbing a ladder, going from the ordinary to the extraordinary, from suffering to bliss. Our first step will be the one that is closest to the ground—our present reality. Unless we take that step and examine our current state, we will not be able to move forward.

Next comes a series of steps that will reveal to you, one by one, the layers of your being. The chapter sequence has been designed to help you achieve this over time. At the highest step of attempting to reveal the ultimate truth, you will get a glimpse of your true nature. Even a fleeting glimpse of that knowledge is enough to help you manage suffering to a great extent. The very process of climbing the ladder empowers you. Even if you do not reach the summit, in terms of realizing the true nature of existence, you will find yourself way ahead of where you are right now. This book aims to reflect the bliss that comes from even a basic understanding of this philosophy. That alone is enough to help yourself out of your misery.

This book values and respects all the other methods that help people deal with their pain and suffering. It does *not* advocate replacing therapy, medicine or counselling with Vedantic understanding. The Vedantic standpoint is panoramic—a view from the highest perspective. Thus, it has space for every method that helps people overcome their pain. Even as you gain a greater understanding of the Vedantic approach to suffering, you must continue with all the other help you can get, be it therapy, medicine or counselling. As you journey through this understanding, you will understand why, for ordinary people like us, practicality and spirituality as two seemingly distinct approaches have to work in conjunction, like the mind and the body.

In order to derive the full benefit of this workbook, it would be best to read the chapters in sequence initially. Unless you think through the significance of each step, skipping chapters will be of little use. Since you are climbing a ladder, you need to ensure a tight grip and a firm footing on each step.

UNIQUE EXERCISES—THE DISTINCTIVE CRUX

To help you find lasting solutions to your problems, this book includes a special feature. It includes practical exercises for you to work on, a game-changer that helps you put the ideas to use, bridging the gap between inspiration and action. Attempting each exercise is of utmost importance in understanding the concepts being presented. Ideally, you should write down the answers, but even if you do not feel like writing them down, say them out loud to yourself, or at least think them over. Come back later and try to write them down. These exercises will make the knowledge work for you, which is the purpose of this workbook.

Once you have read a chapter, mull over the purpose of the exercises. It does not matter how long it takes. The important thing is to understand what the exercise is trying to draw your attention towards. Once you have done the exercises at the end of a chapter (the exercises will begin from Chapter 3), read your answers and ponder over them before moving on to the next chapter.

There are two ways to derive benefits from this workbook. You may go through the entire book in sequence, attempting the exercises at least once as you progress. Once you have gone through the entire workbook, you can come back to the earlier chapters and spend more time on the exercises. Alternatively, you can pause at any section of the book where you need to let the ideas percolate into your mind. Take your time before moving to the next chapter. Also, as you progress through the book, you might want to come back to the previous exercises and do them again.

In life, challenges will keep cropping up. You can come back to this workbook any time, read through the chapters, and attempt the exercises. You will be surprised by how each time you will get fresh insights into your own personality and into the solutions to your problems.

To reach an understanding of what Vedanta is trying to suggest, we first need to understand and evaluate our present state. The philosophy will have to wait for the later chapters, so that we can get comfortable with where we are now in our lives. Let's begin!

2

LET'S FACE IT

Let's cut to the chase. When you are suffering, you do not want a motivational lecture on positive thinking; you want your pain to go away. If you are experiencing extreme pain due to the loss of a loved one or the diagnosis of a serious disease, or if you are facing other challenges like the loss of a job, failure, or even some minor pain, like a little cut on your finger, your entire focus shifts to the pain. Emotional pain hurts, just like physical pain. No amount of positive talk can negate that pain in your mind or body. Neither should the pain be negated. Nature has designed pain for a purpose; else, why would an experience like pain even exist?

Pain is a passageway. It is not an end in itself. It is a part of your life, but it is not your life. Your life has a much larger, more powerful purpose than suffering. Yet, when you have any kind of pain in life, it feels like being trapped in a deep, dark cave. With no exit in sight, and no light at the end of a long dark tunnel, you feel suffocated.

Being in that cave is your reality in those moments and cannot be negated, but your choices make all the difference. You can resign yourself to the situation and stay trapped for the rest of your life, making do with whatever is available in the dark. From then on, your life's components will be customized according to the darkness of the cave. Or, you can try to find a way out, cutting through the rocks and removing the obstacles, to reach an opening where you can step out of that suffocating darkness. For most people, at some stage of suffering, there is a strong desire to come out of the cave. It is in such moments that we start looking for solutions.

Like the innumerable shades of green on this planet, pain too has innumerable forms. When you are feeling low, demotivated, defeated, pained, grief-stricken, or any of the various shades of sadness and you try to look for help, most books, talks and videos seem like superficial talk, mere words. They are attractive, like beautiful works of art that are pleasant to look at, but are of little use in easing your pain. They repeatedly tell you that you can pull yourself out of your suffering. But you are in pain and you do not know how to extricate yourself from it. You feel incapacitated because of your suffering.

YOU MATTER

This book is a companion for your mind and soul, because it is a workbook in which *you* will write. It is first and foremost about *you*, because the primary thing that matters to you is *you*. Suffering is an inseparable part of life, and it is okay to feel pain. What is not okay is to stay in that state of mind.

You owe it to yourself to come out of that state. Your life is a part of an ecosystem that needs you, healthy and strong, whether or not you perceive it that way. You exist for a reason. You are an integral part of this universe and your pain and your happiness matter in the larger scheme of things.

You matter.

This workbook for your mind and soul will work with you to help you transform your pain to bliss. While it is based on the Advaita school of Vedanta, there is nothing particularly religious, racial or community-specific in its approach. That is the beauty of this system of thought—it talks about you as a human being, and guides you through the complexities of life to put you in touch with your deeper reality. It talks to you *about yourself*.

You do not have to be spiritual or religious to access the benefits of Vedanta. Whatever be your inclination—agnosticism, faith, scepticism, atheism, science, logic—your mind is first and foremost a mind. Let's begin the journey by introducing you to your own mind through the deepest insights available to humanity. Let's help you help yourself. Let's emerge from the dark cave into the vibrant garden of life and breathe free.

SHUN THE SHAME-GAME

First things first. Do you know why in times of pain you do not find any solace in the self-help content available around you? That's because most self-help content directly or indirectly blames you for your suffering. That is insensitive. As a society, we humans have generated an ecosystem where we arbitrarily pin all the blame on the sufferer. You are repeatedly told that things are not going right for you because you have a negative mind, or negative thoughts. Just look at all the motivational quotes out there. They scream at you: you are not managing your mind properly, which is why you are suffering. To what degree they are correct is unimportant. What matters is that bombarding you with such ideas sets a guilt trap for you.

How can a person in pain think of anything other than their pain? If something bad has happened to you, your truth for the moment would be the feelings that you are experiencing—distress, guilt, disappointment, or physical pain. Even if you have a toothache, your entire attention is focused on that pain while it lasts. It is difficult to think of anything else. If in such a situation someone tells you to 'think positive', you might want to yell back at them. It is true that your brain focuses on the pain more than on anything else. That is how nature has designed it. It is necessary for survival; else, you will not be able to preserve life in your body. In scientific circles, 'pain is among the most important signals our body gives to help us survive.'[1]

You might know of someone who was suffering but never took professional help because they thought they could handle it on their own. They are not at fault. It is the social framework that shames you for feeling negative emotions. Positive thinking is placed on a pedestal day in and day out. Those of us who are feeling sad just retire into a dark corner and hope for the pain to go away, because we do not want to be seen as weak people whose brains entertain what the world calls negative thoughts.

You might ask, isn't negative thinking a person's fault? Isn't it true that we are not able to manage our mind, which is why we suffer? The answer to these questions is simple: it is wrong to blame an unlit candle for not removing the darkness around it. When you light up the candle, it is inevitable that it will spread light. They tell you that the root of your suffering is that you think negatively, but they do not acquaint you with the fundamentals of the situation.

What is your mind? Did the suffering first arise in the body or in the mind? What do you see when you think of yourself? Is it your physical body or the thoughts in your head, or the reactions and responses that you give to your environment? Or do you visualize yourself as your mind? Think of this: is your mind within you, or is your body within the mind? Can you control the thoughts in your mind? Are you more than your mind?

These questions might seem baffling, especially since not all of us are scientists, philosophers or psychologists. This is where the ancient Indic philosophy known as Advaita Vedanta comes in. It speaks directly to your experience, and addresses these questions in a systematic and user-friendly way, providing unmatched help accessible to every human. It addresses the fundamentals of the problem, and hence offers a very effective way for us to handle our pain and suffering.

WHY VEDANTA?

In contemporary times, when a wealth of psychological and medical guidance is available, why go back to a system of thought that emerged more than 3,000 years ago? To understand this, we need to first quickly explore in brief what Vedanta is.

The term 'Vedanta' means 'the end goal' or 'the highest teaching' of the Vedas. The sacred, revered texts known as the Vedas have embedded within them a corpus of texts known as the Upanishads. The Vedas have many layers, but the Upanishads are different from the other layers in that they are not primarily religious. The Upanishads are logic-based enquiries into the reality of existence. The system of thought elaborated in these texts, together with the Brahma Sutras and the Bhagavad Gita, is known as Vedanta. Vedanta itself can be classified into different schools, but the common goal is to make sense of life, death, and what comes in between.

What sets Vedanta apart from other religious systems is that it does not ask you to have unquestionable faith in any entity. It encourages you to look into your own experience, and to recognize what feels true to you. To achieve this, it talks to you *about yourself*. The aim is to introduce you to what you truly are. It encourages you to ask questions, express doubts, and cross-check your understanding till you reach a stage where you are convinced about the argument being presented. In this sense, the Vedantic quest is like any scientific enquiry. American astronomer-scientist Carl Sagan was probably unaware that his thoughts would echo the very ethos of Vedantic enquiry when he wrote this about the scientific quest: 'Whatever is inconsistent with the facts must be discarded or revised. We must understand the Cosmos as it is and not confuse how it is with how we wish it to be. The obvious is sometimes false; the unexpected is sometimes true.'[2]

It is important to restate that Vedanta empowers you with unparalleled tools to transcend your pain and suffering because it makes you see the core, the seed, the basic facts from which our existence arises. It presents a stark picture of reality. When you know the root of a problem, you are already equipped to cure it.

As a system of thought, Vedanta takes into consideration differing streams and brings them together into a comprehensive analysis, resulting in a unique, powerful insight. It helps you see the truth so directly that you feel extraordinarily empowered. The beauty of this philosophy is that it presents an extraordinary perspective on the nature of reality but with the most ordinary tools.

It is also important to reiterate that the core principles of Vedantic thought are never in conflict with scientific treatment and other methods of healing. On the contrary, Vedanta will show you a way to derive even greater benefit from the healing approaches of modern medicine, psychiatry and psychology.

In the words of the famous nineteenth-century German philosopher Arthur Schopenhauer, 'In the world, there is no study so beautiful and so elevating as the Upanishads. It has been the solace of my life, and will be the solace of my death.'[3]

3

PAIN IS REAL

HAPPINESS IS OVERRATED—DO NOT STRIVE JUST TO BE HAPPY

The human brain experiences more than 6,000 thoughts a day.[1] However, it can effectively process only one thought at a time. In addition, there is something called human brain bandwidth, which is around 40 bits per second. This is slow, really slow processing. To put it in perspective, a computer downloads data at least a million times faster than this.[2] So, when you feel a certain kind of sadness, that is exactly what your brain is processing and projecting as your thoughts. You see those thoughts manifesting as your emotions. If you tried to arbitrarily jump ahead to the 'happiness state', the results would be unpleasant. Such an effort might lead to dissatisfaction and an enhanced feeling of sadness. That would be a guilt trap—you would start blaming yourself for not feeling happy.

Give your brain the space it needs. Process one emotion at a time. Acknowledge the sadness that you feel, and do it without any guilt. The sad state has to be respected, acknowledged; only then can you move forward. If you are standing on the roof of a multi-storey building, and you want to reach the roof of the building across a wide road, you have to first come down to the ground floor of your building, cross the road, and then go up the other building to reach its roof. As ridiculous and tempting as it may sound, you cannot jump across to the other building, unless you have fictional superpowers.

It is fashionable to play the happiness band all the time. The moment you start looking for help, you are burdened with the 'happiness' target. Whether in books, talks, speeches, videos, or other motivational content, you are bombarded with the idea that your aim should be to attain happiness. This expectation is an imposition on you, a directive to ignore whatever you are feeling and to strive for something elusive called happiness. What is worse, it is a presumption that if you are feeling sad, you are doing something wrong, that you are somehow at fault. This is why just striving for 'happiness' is not going to solve your problem.

According to plain logic and, more importantly, according to ancient wisdom, happiness is just *one of the states of the mind*. And a state of mind is *temporary*. Like all other phases, it too shall pass. Recall the last time you were really happy about something. How long did the feeling last? Were you able to hold on to that state of mind permanently?

WHAT WE CAN ACHIEVE

Here is a necessary disclaimer. We are not talking about avoiding happiness. We are not talking about wallowing in sadness. On the contrary, we are talking about reaching a state of lasting bliss that goes beyond temporary bursts of happiness. It is that state where your mind is so calm that joy does not uproot you and sadness does not disturb you. It is that state of mind where you are happy in the purest form, without the fear of losing happiness, even when you face sad times in your life.

In case you think this is a lofty state possible only for yogis or monks, that is a misconception. You can carry on with your life and ambitions normally, and still reach that state of calm. We might not be able to perfect this state, but without a doubt, we all can reach a stage where we can experience lasting bliss and not just a temporary happy state.

Vedanta does not ask you to negate your emotions. It acknowledges them. Then, in sublime poetry and meticulous explanations, it tells you that however sad you may be currently, it is certain that you will ultimately reach a state of bliss. The reason for this, according to the Upanishads, is simple—your very nature is bliss; you just do not recognize it yet. This underlying idea resonates across all Vedantic texts. The Taittiriya Upanishad mentions: 'They knew Bliss as Brahman; for from Bliss, indeed, all these beings originate; having been born, they are sustained by Bliss; they move towards and merge in Bliss.'[3]

That unchanging bliss is your deepest reality, your true nature. Whatever transient emotions you might feel right now, you can go back to your original state of pure bliss. Does that sound too improbable or theoretical? As you go through various stages of this workbook, you will uncover the hidden aspects of your own being, and there will be many surprises on the way. As the first step in that direction, let's help you listen to your own mind.

LET IT OUT

This is the space where you will spend some much-needed time with yourself. Sit in a quiet place where you can think without distraction for a few minutes. Read the questions below slowly. Understand each question and then write down whatever comes to your mind as an answer. If you like, you may write in this space, or if you need to elaborate further, you may use a dedicated additional notebook or a diary for this purpose. Your answers need not be perfectly written. Just write down the words that come to your mind as you think things through. Though writing the answers would be ideal, if you do not like to write, you can say the answers out loud. If you feel like expressing yourself in another language, go ahead. Just remember, do not hold back anything. This is the space to let out all that you are feeling.

EXERCISE: YOUR THOUGHTS ARE IMPORTANT

a) What is making you sad right now? Is it a physical problem, an emotional situation or mental stress of any kind? It could be a combination of these. Your physical pain could be causing you mental stress, or your emotional pain could be affecting your ability to physically function to full capacity. Write down which of these states you think you are experiencing.

_____
_____
_____
_____
_____
_____

b) Close your eyes after reading the following. Imagine a trusted friend sitting next to you. That friend could be another person, or it could be you yourself, in which case, imagine yourself talking to your reflection in the mirror and treat your reflection as your closest friend. When your visualization is steady, open your eyes and write the answers to the following questions as if you are answering your friend. Write the name of whom you are talking to.

_____

_____

c) Where are you hurting? Is the pain in some part of your body, your mind, or both?

_____

_____

d) How are you feeling about this pain?

_____

_____

_____

_____

e) Have you felt like this before? Once? Many times?

_____

_____

_____

_____

_____

_____

f) How did it start this time?

___

g) Do you blame someone for this?

___

h) Do you want this state to continue or would you like it to end? Why?

___

After you have answered all the questions above, go over them. Think about what you have written, about your dialogue with yourself. Do this before moving to the next chapter. Now, when you have expressed how you feel about your pain, let's take you to the next step.

4

SEPARATE THE PAIN FROM THE SUFFERING

PAIN IS CERTAIN BUT SUFFERING IS A CHOICE

Here is something that is crucial to helping you deal with your suffering. Pain and suffering are not the same. Pain is what happened to you, whether physical or mental. Suffering arises from your response to it. Think of your answers to the questions at the end of Chapter 3. The location of your pain, whether physical or emotional, is tangible. You can point out if you are hurt emotionally, or if there is an unpleasant sensation in any part of the body. Now think of this: the pain itself is not causing you the suffering. Your interpretation of that pain results in your suffering. What you feel about the event that caused the pain, and how you presume you should react to that event, form the basis of whether or not you will suffer. Differentiating between pain and suffering is important but the concept might be a little difficult to grasp.

As if to illustrate this point, at times humanity

witnesses individuals who not only understand but also beautifully demonstrate this differentiation through the way they live their lives. One such outstanding example is Stephen Hawking, one of the most brilliant physicists and cosmologists to have lived in our times, the man whose research revolutionized the way we understand our universe, especially black holes.

At the age of 21, when Hawking, a promising doctoral scholar, was not only looking forward to an exciting career, but was also engaged to be married soon, he was diagnosed with a rare, crippling motor neuron disease and was given only about two more years to live. This disease, known as amyotrophic lateral sclerosis (ALS) or Lou Gehrig's disease, is a cruel, slow-progressing disease that gradually paralyses a person's entire body, affecting the motor functions of all the muscles, and finally turns fatal. Within a few years of the diagnosis, Hawking was wheelchair-bound, having lost all movement in almost all parts of his body. What makes this disease even worse is the fact that the mind of the person remains active; hence, Hawking witnessed each part of his body becoming dysfunctional one by one.

As if this was not enough, he contracted life-threatening pneumonia some years later, and to save his life, a tracheostomy had to be done, which basically involves inserting a pipe through the throat to enable breathing. As a result of the procedure, he lost his speech completely.

For the rest of his life, he could communicate only through a specially customized computer. Initially, he could press a button to select one word at a time. These were converted by the computer into sentences. The speed was around 15 words per minute. To add to the problem, he soon lost the functioning of the muscles in the hand too. After that, he selected words by twitching some facial muscles, and the selected words were converted into an electronic voice. The speed of selection slowed down to one word per minute. It took a painstakingly long time for him to communicate even a simple sentence. In addition, there were other health challenges throughout his life.

How he dealt with this immense pain, from that young age to the age of 76 when he passed away, is astonishing to say the least. He kept working on the most intense, highly specialized research topics with leading physicists throughout the world, and kept collecting medals, awards and accolades. Besides his groundbreaking research that was the highlight of his life, he also became somewhat of a pop icon, appearing in several television series, notably *Star Trek* and *The Simpsons*.* Moreover, he lent his unique mechanical voice to musical albums too. His persona was depicted in a number of movies, shows and animated series. That he looked different from 'normal' people, with his head tilted and face contorted, and that he had to use an electric wheelchair, never diminished his zest for life.

If that was not amazing enough, he travelled the world, addressing the scientific community, flew in a hot-air balloon on his sixtieth birthday, and took a zero-gravity flight at the age of 65. He was also a bestselling author who played a pioneering role in popularizing science, and his books remain among the most read in the genre of popular science.

---

*One episode as Professor Stephen Hawking in *Star Trek: The Next Generation* (1993) and a voice role in four episodes of *The Simpsons* (1999–2010).

If you think you would have seen him grim-faced all the time, you are mistaken. Hawking was known to have a canny sense of humour, cracking a joke every now and then. He even planned to fly to space one day. In the words of prominent American physicist Michio Kaku, 'Not since Albert Einstein has a scientist so captured the public imagination and endeared himself to tens of millions of people around the world.'[1]

How did Hawking manage to do so much in a life of unimaginable pain? Was it easy for him? No. When he was diagnosed with Lou Gehrig's disease, he said that it came as a shock to him and that it was a difficult time for him. But as he accepted his condition, he never allowed the pain to get converted into suffering. In his own words, 'It is a waste of time to be angry about my disability. One has to get on with life and I haven't done badly. People will not have time for you if you are always angry or complaining.'[2] He explained in another interview, 'I relish the rare opportunity I've been given to live the life of the mind. But I know I need my body and that it will not last forever.'[3] Another quote from him goes: 'I want to show that people need not be limited by physical handicaps as long as they are not disabled in spirit.'[4]

His colleague, Cambridge cosmologist Martin Rees, summed up Stephen Hawking's life in these words: 'What a triumph his life has been. His name will live in the annals of science; millions have had their cosmic horizons widened by his best-selling books; and even more, around the world, have been inspired by a unique example of achievement against all the odds—a manifestation of amazing willpower and determination.'[5]

YOU TOO CAN DO IT

While Stephen Hawking's condition was extraordinary, many of us get distressed even when we just have a sore throat. Someone says a rude word to us and we give in to anger or distress. The truth about these situations will remain unchanged—if the throat is infected, it will cause discomfort. Rude words will feel unpleasant. Yet, it is our choice whether or not we want to suffer because of these situations.

To reinforce that point, let's take a hypothetical situation. Imagine that for the past two months, you have been looking forward to a party with old friends, something that has not happened for years. You have a long list of memories that you want to revisit with them. But a few hours before leaving, you twist your ankle. The pain is intense and the doctor prescribes bed rest.

There can be two ways to react to this situation. You may feel miserable, and declare that your life is wretched. You may imagine the fun the other people will be having in the party. You may think that no one will miss you, and that no one cares about you. You may lament your fate—how wasteful it was to prepare for the party and why, after everything, did this have to happen and at such a time. You may even be convinced that there is no point looking forward to anything in life.

Alternatively, you can focus on the fact that your ankle is hurt and that you need to rest. You may feel disappointed about not attending the party, but the disappointment does not make you feel bad about yourself or your life. You remain aware of how much pain there is, whether it is getting better or worse, or if you need an ice pack or a painkiller. However, you do not connect the pain to the idea that your life is wretched because you are disappointed. In this case, you might focus on healing speedily, and you might even think of finding other ways of meeting the people you wanted to. You might want to go a step ahead and use that rest time to catch up on something for which you usually do not have time, like watching a series or reading a book.

Yet, if you generally tend to replicate the pattern of the first option, do not blame yourself. The difference between positive and negative thinking is not much. Pain is not always perceived in black and white. It is a result of a thousand complex phenomena in your brain. It is more about how you perceive yourself in relation to pain. Come to think of it, where was the pain? In the ankle. But in the first case, you magnified that pain into suffering and in the second case, you accepted the pain and held the suffering at bay.

YOU HAVE A CHOICE

The situation repeats itself through every experience in life—when someone hurts you emotionally, when you fail a test, when you have a headache, when you are diagnosed with a disease, or in extreme cases, when you lose a loved one. In each case, the pain is real. But your suffering depends on how you think about that pain. The pain is *not a choice*, but suffering *is a choice*.

Human life inevitably brings with it many challenges. The list is endless. Ironically, all of us envision only a perfect life, with no pain, no disease, no hurt, no loss. We live in denial of reality—where there is life, there will be pain.

But here is the game-changing perspective: your pain need not make you suffer. Your pain need not make you sad. Every time someone or something hurts you, you have the choice either to transform your pain into suffering or to not do so.

Here is a method to help you differentiate between pain and suffering whenever the situation arises. Think of pain at two levels: physical and emotional. For instance, a bruise, a fracture, a fever, and the like, cause pain in a certain part of the body. Emotional pain such as fear, disgust, jealousy, guilt and more is a result of biochemical processes in your brain. However, in both situations the pain gets converted into suffering only in your mind. For instance, the rude behaviour of a person towards you is out there, in the physical world. That behaviour needs to be tackled, but if you start thinking about it, or derive conclusions about yourself by thinking about it, you are converting the pain into suffering. This is because you are giving that person and their toxicity a home in your head. To prevent that, you can restrict your pain to the specific facts of the situation. You can keep your mind clear of any interpretations of those events, while working to cure the pain.

THE BUDDHA'S TWO ARROWS

This age-old secret of the two levels of suffering has an explanation in a famous Buddhist parable entitled the 'Two Arrows of Suffering'.[6] Gautama Buddha, when talking to his disciples, explained that having pain in life is like being struck with two arrows. If a person is struck with an arrow, they will be in pain, but if another arrow strikes the person, the suffering will increase manifold.

The first arrow is the pain that is a part of life. That includes grief, anger, misfortune, disease, old age and physical pain. These are inevitable. However, what would it be like to be in this pain and be struck by a second arrow? The second arrow, according to the Buddha, is our reaction to the pain that life gives us. We can always prevent shooting ourselves with the second arrow because *that is optional*. The first arrow in this case is the pain that life brings with it, and we have no control over it. However, we can have complete control over the second arrow, and that is the one where most of the suffering lies. Would you hurt yourself even more when you are already in pain?

SOME GRIM SITUATIONS

At times, it becomes difficult to practise separating pain from suffering. A person mourning the death of a loved one is in the most intense pain imaginable. That vacuum in their life can never be filled. The bereaved person faces a range of emotions from anger to helplessness. They will and should express their emotions to whoever they are comfortable with. The loss is real and the person has every right to feel grief.

Yet, the suffering can broadly take two forms. The bereaved person may be broken, feel incapacitated and be unable to carry on their normal life. In this case, they will become a burden to their family. Alternatively, the grieving person may transform their suffering into a loving tribute to the deceased person. One way of doing this is by making a mental album of all the happy times spent with the deceased, or by recollecting the good things the deceased had done in their life. Recollecting either or both gives meaning and purpose to the life of the deceased. The suffering is then converted into something graceful rather than something unbearable.

Here would come a natural objection: what about the death of a child, or the untimely accidental death of a young person, for instance? What about a martyred soldier's family? What about a little child with a terminal disease or a child born with a disability? What about people losing their family or their life's earnings in natural calamities such as an earthquake? The suffering in these cases is agonizing. The family and friends want answers as to why this misfortune had to befall them. At such times, those who believe in God lose their faith, while those who are otherwise optimistic about life start questioning the fairness of it all.

The truth is that no one has the answers to such questions. Religion tries to offer some answers, but they are not always reassuring. For those in pain, such reassurances and explanations seem irrelevant; nothing seems to work. The only way to manage such suffering can be summed up in one word: acceptance. It might take time, but if there is no acceptance, the pain of the loss will grow into agonizing, prolonged suffering. If there is gradual acceptance of what has happened, even though the 'why' cannot be answered, the suffering will not incapacitate the person.

There are other emotional states that are as distressing as grief, such as those provoked by betrayal, cheating, body-shaming, being defamed or framed. While the pain from these could be as intense as losing someone, it is comparatively easier to manage suffering in such cases. That is because it is easy to see what was done *to* you. It was someone else's actions. You are still in control of how you react to that situation. Every time you face such a situation, practise separating pain from suffering. At first, it will not be easy, but even if you make some effort to separate the two, you will have progressed.

EXERCISE: LET'S PRACTISE BY VISUALIZING

a) Recall any time in your past when you had an injury on any part of your body. It could have been a cut, a bruise, a fracture, or anything that caused you pain. Recall the incident and write down your responses to the following questions:

How did you get the injury?

_____
_____
_____
_____

Did you feel like blaming someone?

_____
_____
_____
_____

How intense was the pain?

_____
_____
_____
_____

What were the thoughts that crossed your mind on getting hurt?

When you were in pain, did it affect your interaction with other people?

b) Now travel back in time to the same situation. This time, your effort will be to keep the pain and the suffering separate. Visualize the entire scene in your mind and modify your responses to tell yourself that you accept the pain but you choose not to suffer. Recall the incident, but this time, whenever the pain triggers a negative thought that makes you suffer, stop the thought right away. This is going to be your mantra: 'I refuse to give power to the pain to make me suffer.' Write down an entire new narrative of the same incident using this mantra. Start from the moment of getting hurt, and write in detail all the thoughts that would have crossed your mind. Let it flow like a story.

_____
_____
_____
_____
_____
_____
_____

After you have completed the above two exercises, go over your answers. Compare how the two reactions were different. Tell yourself that the next time a similar injury happens, you will let the pain be wherever it is. You will not allow it to take the form of suffering. Once you have repeated this to yourself, move on to the next chapter.

5

YOU ARE NOT YOUR PAIN

> One equal temper of heroic hearts,
> Made weak by time and fate, but strong in will
> To strive, to seek, to find, and not to yield.[1]

Alfred, Lord Tennyson's legendary poem 'Ulysses' (1833) celebrates living life to the fullest. Beyond that, this poem is a sublime depiction of a human being's accomplishment of keeping his suffering separate from his inner self. Old king Ulysses, who is now weaker in body, and has experienced not just glory but also numerous setbacks in life, is not ready to give up just yet. What is remarkable is that he wants to take on more challenges, not because of any obligation, but to celebrate life itself, 'to drink life to the lees'.[2] Nothing can deter him from exploring more, neither the challenges of old age, nor the formidable dangers faced in the past. Whatever misery he has faced in the past is now a source of strength for him, because it has made him understand life better. What is the difference between him and others who give up after the slightest experience of misery? He sees problems in the external situations, not in himself. Since he can separate himself from the suffering caused by the pain, he is undaunted by both.

Like Ulysses, you can differentiate between what is happening to you and what you allow to affect you. That is the difference between pain and suffering, which leads us to the next crucial step. Pain is something that happens *to* you. It is not you. When you are in pain, whether emotional or physical, it seems that your existence is intricately interwoven with the despair that you experience. If you look closely, you will observe that though your body or mind is in pain, there is still a distance between you and the pain or suffering. You *experience* pain. This is the master key to alleviating your pain and suffering. However, to fully grasp its significance, we need to take some more steps.

YOUR PAIN CANNOT DEFINE YOU

Here is the story of the legendary Chinese entrepreneur, Ma Yun, better known as Jack Ma, whose entire life is a lesson in how you can face suffering, yet never be affected by it.

Since childhood, Jack Ma faced challenges. Ma grew up in poverty, bullied and body-shamed for his bony and skinny looks, something that continued into the later part of his life as well. Growing up in politically sensitive China in the 1970s was not easy either. His saving grace could have been academics but he was not conventionally good at school and failed multiple times at various exams. When it was time to apply to college, he failed the entrance test miserably, not once but twice. In the compulsory subject mathematics, that required a minimum of seventy marks, he scored just one. He started doing odd jobs like transporting magazines on his bicycle, while preparing to take the exam again. In the second attempt, he scored a mere nineteen marks in mathematics. One of his teachers remarked that if Ma cleared the college entrance test, he would 'start writing his name upside down'.[3] When Ma made up his mind to get just any job instead, including the job of a waiter, he was rejected from no less than thirty places.

While he was officially declared a failure, even by his parents, Ma did not let the extreme discouragement stop him. He kept studying at night, while doing odd jobs by day. He refused to be defeated on the inside, and that was crucial. His focus was on persevering himself, rather than letting criticism affect him. On the sidelines, he pursued his passion for learning English. This simple self-acquired skill turned out to be a key factor in his success later. Seemingly defeated on the outside, but undeterred inside, Ma took the entrance exam a third time…and he cleared the exam.

His troubles, however, were not over. Professional challenges had just begun. He could secure admission only in an ordinary college, and trained to be a teacher. Yet, Ma kept dreaming big and learning continuously. He tried his hand at some ventures after college, but it was after much struggle that he finally started doing what he had always dreamt of.

His vision of building a technology company in China was materialized when he built one of the biggest technology conglomerates in the world, providing employment to millions of people and forever changing the commercial landscape of his country. Nothing, however, came easy to him. At every step, there were huge setbacks and discouragement.

When he spoke to Western businesses about his ideas, he was termed 'crazy Jack' for dreaming beyond his means.[4] He was mocked at for taking on a Goliath, eBay, the largest e-commerce company at that time. However, with consistent effort and smart decisions, he reduced eBay's market share from 90 per cent to a mere 7 per cent in just three years, forcing them to quit the Chinese market.[5] Venture capitalists in America who had dismissed him (around thirty of them had rejected his proposals) saw Ma's IPO creating history in 2014 when it became the biggest IPO till then—bigger than the combined might of Facebook, Twitter (now X) and Google.[6]

How could this ordinary person rise above all the miseries that life continued to heap on him? What if he had allowed each challenge to create hell in his mind? The story would have been one of suffering and failure. Therein lies the difference. Ma was not ready to suffer because of the pain that situations brought him. He knew that the situations were out there, but it was his choice whether to let them affect him or not. This fine discernment was responsible for Jack Ma becoming one of the most iconic figures in modern history.

TYPES OF SUFFERING

It is possible for you, too, to separate your pain from yourself. You need to remind yourself that the problems are happening *to* you; hence they cannot define you. Through millennia, humankind has tried to understand various aspects of pain and suffering. Religion, philosophy, science and, in recent times, even pop culture have tried to debate the nuances.

A particularly interesting classification of suffering appears in ancient texts.[7] While something as abstract as suffering cannot have an all-encompassing description, the attempt in these texts is not to give a comprehensive account. The purpose of the classification is to underscore that suffering is always external to our true selves, to make us see how it is possible to detach ourselves from the sorrow that comes our way.

To help us with this, the Samkhya Karika, composed around 300 CE, mentions suffering to be broadly of three types. The first one is called *adhyatmika dukkha* or problems one faces in the body and mind. This includes physical pain such as injuries, diseases or handicaps. Mental illnesses, depression, distress, and a range of negative emotions also fall into this category.

The second one is called *adibhautika dukkha* or suffering due to 'other beings'. These other creatures could be organisms like mosquitoes and bacteria that cause bodily suffering. Danger from wild animals, as was a reality in ancient times, is included in this type. It exists to some extent in modern times as well. The coronavirus that caused an unprecedented pandemic is supposed to have been originally present in wild bats, but was passed on to some unidentified animal carrier, and finally transmitted to humans.

This type of misery also includes suffering caused by other humans, which is ironically the larger reality in modern times. Wars, persecution, genocide and discrimination are the darkest forms of this suffering inflicted by humans on their own species. There are other aspects of suffering as well, ranging from apathy to deliberately hurting others.

The third type of suffering is called *adidaivika dukkha*

or suffering caused by supernatural forces—floods, earthquakes, landslides, cyclones and the various other powerful forces of nature. The suffering caused by these agencies seems to be the handiwork of powers greater than human beings. Often, the pain inflicted through these means leaves us confused and makes us question the fairness of life.

The classification can be open to debate, but that is not the purpose. If you look closely—and this is important—whatever be the source of pain, it did not originate in you, not even the mental distress. It is your reaction to pain that results in suffering.

To understand how you can separate yourself from your pain, please do the following exercises.

EXERCISE 1: THE BAG METHOD

Read through this exercise, understand the requirement, and then sit in a comfortable position, preferably in a place without distractions. Then close your eyes and follow the steps mentioned below:

1. Breathe normally. Notice your breath entering and leaving your system.
2. Keeping your eyes closed, move your fingers. Close your hands and open them. Feel the sensation of your fingers and thumbs as you close and open your hands. Then rest your hands.
3. Now pay attention to the thoughts that you are having. Notice where you feel your thoughts. It could be somewhere in your head, behind your eyes, or in your chest area.

4. Now, imagine the thoughts as things, tangible objects that you can touch and grab. You might find a crowd of thoughts in that visualization. These could be frustration, anger, pity or guilt, for instance. Look at them. Give them names, colours or shapes if you want.
5. Now imagine a bag that is outside of you—a sack, a purse, a polybag, anything.
6. Locate the thought that is troubling you the most. Mentally pick it up and put it into the bag. Put another thought if you want. Take a deep breath of satisfaction as you get rid of each thought. For example, if you have dumped the feeling of guilt into the bag, take a deep breath and tell yourself that you have discarded the unwanted thought.
7. Relax and visualize the unwanted thoughts that you have discarded into the bag. Tell yourself that if you want, you can pick up a troublesome thought again and put it back into your mind. However, tell yourself that you do not want it.

After you have completed the visualization, write down any part of the experience that you want to. Acknowledge your feelings to yourself. You need not have done it perfectly, but if you even tried, write down how you feel about it. You may repeat this exercise as many times as you want.

_____
_____
_____
_____
_____
_____

EXERCISE 2: THE DISTANCE METHOD

This method is designed to help you throughout life, no matter the circumstances in which you find yourself. You can invoke this method whenever you feel your mind is troubled, or you experience suffering of any kind. You may want to do this by sitting down in a quiet place, or even while you are on the go.

See yourself in your mind as if you are watching yourself from a distance. In other words, consider yourself to be another person. Then, watch 'them' reacting to pain. Be straightforward in telling 'them' how they are reacting. Try to advise 'them' how to handle the situation. Address 'them' by name, and give suggestions. When you see yourself from a detached perspective, you will be surprised to learn how meaningful your suggestions can be. When you open your eyes, remind yourself of the suggestions, as if you are still watching the 'other person'. You may want to write down the entire narrative, the setting, the dialogue and your feelings in the space below.

_____

_____

_____

_____

_____

Note: At this stage, two things might happen. Either you will succeed in separating yourself from the pain whenever it arises, or you will have an idea of what you should do. Both possibilities are important next steps. Even if you have tried, it is good progress. We do not expect a complete solution at this step. Let's try to make the path smoother.

6

WHAT ARE YOU?

Here comes the most intriguing part of the journey. In the attempt to try to see your pain as separate from yourself, this question invariably arises—what exactly am I? What is it that we are referring to as 'me' or 'myself'? Do you visualize yourself as this body of yours, as you think you appear to other people, or do you think of yourself as your mind? Should you define yourself by your personality? Or, do you visualize yourself as a mind–body with a soul somewhere within the body?

You might be frustrated by the question 'What exactly am I?' After all, we spend our lives expressing ourselves in terms of I, me, my, mine, myself, etc. We think we know ourselves. You might say that the answer to the question is simply that you are a combination of mind and body. Or, more likely, you will want to dismiss this question as unnecessary. Most of us do not even want to consider this rather irrelevant-sounding query. It appears to be dry philosophy, riddled with impractical assumptions and claims that have nothing to do with everyday life.

But is that so? What if this is the most important question of your life?

WHY THE QUESTION IS IMPORTANT

We get on with our lives, chasing desires and dreams, living under the wishful assumption that only pleasant experiences should come our way. Even when we see the suffering of others, we think it is for them, not for us. We go through life in denial of its darker aspects, especially disease and death. These presumptions, however, are shattered in moments of distress or misfortune. As much as we would like to close our eyes to it, pain in one form or the other will come to us too. It is during such times that we ask: 'Why me?' or 'Why this?' or 'Why now?' In the darkest times, like the death of a loved one, the 'why' assumes monstrous proportions. It haunts us and makes us question the very raison d'être of existence, of life. We begin to think that when everyone has to die, why should there be any life at all? What is the point of going through pain and suffering only to die in the end?

To understand this, we need to get to the depths of the reasons behind life and death. For that, we need to first understand what we actually are. What is it within us that is the real us? Do we really die? Is this life real or is this just a holographic projection? What if all this is just a dream? These are questions that we usually dismiss as unnecessary, but deep down in these questions lie the solutions to our problems.

Our unwillingness to explore our reality is the root of all our suffering, which is why it is all-important to understand what we are. How can we treat something when we do not know what it is? Simply put, to solve the problem of suffering, we need to understand *what* is affecting *whom*. In the exercises at the end of the previous chapter, you might have observed how it is sometimes a struggle to remove pain from yourself because you cannot specify the locus of your true self. You might sometimes think that the real you is in the heart, or in the mind, or somewhere in your head.

The task of keeping your pain separate from you becomes easier when you know what you are referring to when you think of 'I'. To really resolve the problem of pain and suffering, it is imperative to clarify what we are referring to when we refer to ourselves.

COMMON NOTIONS

The biggest challenge is that when we try to express what we think we are, words do not seem adequate. The concept itself seems confusing, even unnecessary. Most of us, when faced with this, would answer along one of the following lines mentioned below.

Identity

We commonly identify ourselves according to the roles we have in life. That answers the question *who* you are, but does not answer *what* you are. This identification could be at a personal level—mother, father, son, daughter. More commonly, we identify ourselves according to the work we do—teacher, student, doctor, scientist, plumber, social worker—in short, whatever work is the primary area of our activity. Even in our education system, the entire race is to inspire people to become 'somebody' rather than a 'nobody'. Yet, what we are racing towards is just a role, a temporary role needed to sustain our lives. What is it that is chasing those roles? What are you, if you are not in that role?

Divisions

Very often, at the next level, we define ourselves according to our culture, geography or beliefs. You might identify as Indian, American or South African. That is your nationality, based on the political divisions of our world. Even if you are deeply patriotic, you are not just a citizen of a particular country. You are more than that—you are an inhabitant of the planet. Likewise, describing yourself according to your religion or as a follower of a faith cannot be your sole identity. If some technology could remove the memory of your faith and your country from your brain, you would still exist. What is it then that you are beyond these identities?

Species

Many believe that we should identify ourselves only as humans. This is a noble thought that can provide the foundation for world peace and progress. It can help us live more empathetically and in harmony with people across the globe. But that still does not answer our question. Let's focus on any individual human. How do we define a human? Are they the body, the mind, or just a creature with the most developed brain in the solar system? If all of us are humans, why are we not able to have an empathetic attitude towards each other? Why do we hate? Why do we think some of us are better than the others? Why do we strive to prove our supremacy over other humans? Why do we wage wars and justify them? Clearly, the identity of being a human is not sufficient for most of us.

The Mind

Most of us realize that apart from our external, superficial identities, we are something more substantial on the inside. To the world, you might be the sum total of the aforementioned external identities, but when you are alone with yourself, you know deep inside that the thoughts in your head are a truer version of what you actually are. We generally live at two levels—that of the external presentations and that of the inner world of the mind.

The mind is difficult to describe. A collective of factors, it includes thoughts, intellect, memories, emotions, desires, etc. Within that paradigm, we define ourselves differently. You might want to say that someone is a good person, or a brilliant thinker. We use numerous such identities when we define people according to their minds—a crooked person, a psychopath, a saint, an adventure seeker, a compassionate soul, a go-getter...the list is endless.

Yet, even that does not provide the complete picture. We often do not identify ourselves with the world on the basis of our inner world. So, we end up creating a mixed description of our roles and our predominant mental characteristics.

Personality

That is where personality comes into the picture. The term 'personality' is an aggregate of your thoughts, behaviour, attitudes and your general way of thinking. This is the aspect of our lives that we are most concerned about presenting to the world. For instance, having a particular personality makes you a good leader; another personality type would make you a fine manager, and so on. Our personalities affect many areas of our lives, from personal relationships to professional success. That is why there is great focus on personality enhancement. Personality development, a $50-billion-plus industry in 2024, is expected to almost double in size in the next ten years.[1]

Let's look at this aspect closely. Your personality is the sum total of your way of thinking and how that translates into your behaviour. In other words, it is an expression of how your inner world reflects in your outward dealings with the world. But is that the whole story? Is that the real you? The personality is just one of the ways in which you appear to yourself and to the world. It is not your entire reality.

That leads us back to where we began. It is a conundrum. We definitely feel that we should define ourselves with an identity, either as a part of a group or as a particular personality. None of these still answers the question—what exactly are you? Let's now climb the next step of the ladder to unravel this mystery. But before we take that step, the following exercise will help condition your mind.

EXERCISE

This exercise will help you a) gauge what level of understanding you currently have of yourself, and b) get in touch with the conscious and subconscious ideas in your mind, before we set off on the path of Vedantic self-enquiry.

Sit in a quiet place in a comfortable position. Breathe normally. Close your eyes after reading through this paragraph and record your experience later. When you close your eyes, draw your attention to different parts of your body—your toes, your fingers, your stomach and the like. Feel that those organs are a part of you.

Draw your attention to your face. Keeping your eyes closed, become aware of your facial features—your lips, your nose, your eyes and your cheeks. You will find yourself visualizing your face as you see it in the mirror. Move away from that image and feel your face directly for yourself, by moving your lips, your nose and your eyes. Experience them directly, without a mirror.

Now bring your thoughts to what you feel is inside your body—the beating of your heart, your breath entering your chest, the movement of your eyes behind the eyelids, the blood flowing through your body. Think of other images of your body, external or internal.

Next, shift your attention to the thoughts in your mind. Do not try to control the thoughts; let them come and go. Just observe what your mind is thinking. Where are those thoughts? Are they in your brain? Are all of those thoughts a part of you?

Now, try to bring it all together and think of yourself as a collective of all these parts—the external organs of your body, the inner body, and your mind. When you have visualized all of the above, open your eyes gently and write down your thoughts about this experience.

You do not have to form concrete observations. Just recall what you felt about these visualizations. These could be random observations. For example, you could have felt that we often do not pay attention to what is inside our bodies. You might also not want to think of the inner organs. Just recognize they are there. Similarly, when you 'saw' your thoughts floating in your mind, what was your reaction? Observe and record whatever you feel about this entire exercise. There are no perfect answers, only your subjective observations.

You may repeat this as many times as you want, but do it comprehensively at least once before moving to the next chapter.

_____
_____
_____
_____
_____
_____
_____
_____
_____
_____

7
THE PATH TO FINDING THE ANSWERS

'O adorable sir, which is that thing, which having been known, all this becomes known?'[1] In the Mundaka Upanishad, a householder named Shaunaka, desirous of understanding this mystery, approaches the great sage Angiras and asks this question. His query represents a universal quest in the minds of each of us who are facing adversities and trying to make sense of life. This defining of what we are is also the quintessential question that has haunted humankind since the ancient times, because it holds the key to understanding suffering. Across cultures, space and time, different disciplines focusing on understanding the human condition have put forth their own set of answers, ranging from reductionist biochemistry to surreal ideas of soul and spirit.

Scientific or philosophical explanations, however, are not our direct experiences when we are going about our everyday lives. In our common understanding, we believe that it is only people with the deepest insights—mystics, saints or accomplished scientists—who understand the mysteries of life. We give up even before we begin. That closes doors for us, doors that can lead us to a view of the real scenario, and can make all the difference to our lives.

Yet, there is a way to understand these things simply by looking closely at our everyday experiences. That is the way of Vedanta. Vedanta talks so directly to us that it is possible to validate its claims with ordinary experiences. It is important to mention here that the primary aim of Vedantic study is to attain the highest spiritual goals—to help us perceive the ultimate reality and to uncover the secrets of the cosmos; in other words, to become enlightened.

While reaching that ultimate reality requires extraordinary focus and determination, for worldly humans like us, even a preliminary understanding of this great mystery can create magic in our lives. Even if we acquire a simple understanding of what this philosophy is trying to point towards, we will be empowered with a solution to end our suffering. That understanding is like a key to a treasure. Once we have the key, it is up to us to use it to unlock the doors that separate us from the treasure.

So, what is that enigmatic reality of life, whose knowledge and understanding will forever relieve us of our pain and suffering? Let us move further into this realm of the mystery that is at once evident, yet hidden from our sight.

IS REALITY KNOWABLE?

If you give some thought to the idea of an ultimate reality, you will immediately come up with two observations. First, isn't reality evident? What we see and perceive in the world is reality, isn't it? Second, if our true nature is hidden, and if it was at all knowable, wouldn't we have already known it? We are creatures with the most sophisticated brains in the universe. We would assume that we are intuitively capable of understanding what we are. If not intuitively, then our study of the world would have led us to it by now.

Very likely, you might think you already have the answer: that a human is a sum of their parts—mind, body, and soul, as you might have felt in the exercise in the previous chapter. But a sum of parts is an aggregate; it is not a unity. What is that one thing that holds those parts together? What is that one thing that makes any entity sentient?

What the Upanishads explain is as stunning as it is surreal in poetic expression. These texts say that reality is not only knowable, but it is very much accessible and available to all, at all times. 'That highest Bliss is located in one's own Self,' says sixth-century philosopher-saint Gaudapada in his *karika* on the Mandukya Upanishad.[2] The Kena Upanishad mentions mysteriously, 'It is really known when It is known with each state of consciousness.'[3] That means the ultimate reality is evident in each experience of ours, in each action, each moment in time. Yet, it is known when it is recognized. The word 'recognized' is crucial because that reality is so close to us that it cannot be found or searched for; it can only be recognized. It is our truest nature, and we *are it* all the time. Yet, we fail to see our true selves. If we *are* that reality at all times, why are we not aware of it?

THE OPEN SECRET

Now, here is an astonishing claim. We cannot see our true nature right now because it is hidden behind a veil.

Our perception of reality, moulded by the conditioning of our minds, keeps this truth hidden from us. This veil is not an external agent; it is not an object or an invisible power. Surprisingly, it is nothing but our ignorance. Our being oblivious to the reality is the entire problem. Swami Vivekananda called this an 'open secret'. 'Whichever way we turn in trying to understand things in their reality, if we analyze far enough, we find that at last we come to a peculiar state of things, seemingly a contradiction: something which our reason cannot grasp and yet is a fact.'[4]

As we progress further with this book, we will slowly unpack the lofty expressions of the Upanishadic texts that give us a clear picture of that truth hidden behind the veil. That would answer all our questions, from the nature of our self to the workings of this universe. And when we get that clear picture, pain and suffering will become easier to handle. To begin with, here is a little glimpse into what our true self is like.

The Isha Upanishad casts a net of mystery on our understanding in this famous verse: 'That moves, That does not move; That is far off, That is very near; That is inside all this, and That is also outside all this.'[5] Though it is not possible to explain the entire import of this verse in a few words, let us understand for now that the seemingly paradoxical nature of our reality, which sounds so confusing, is explained in pairs of opposites because the ultimate reality is all-encompassing. The paradoxes resolve themselves in one reality.

Again, the Katha Upanishad says, 'It is hidden in all beings, and hence It does not appear as the Self of all. But by the seers of subtle things, It is seen through a pointed and fine intellect.'[6] The sharp intellect being referred to here is a broad-based term, which includes our desire to understand the truth and the effort we make for it. But the message is reassuring. Our true nature, though not apparent, can be perceived in all of us.

In order to understand what these intriguing statements mean, let's go from the sublime poetry of the Upanishads to a mundane example. You know you have a face. This statement might seem bizarre, but try and understand what it means. How do you know you have a face? Probably because when you look into a mirror, you see what your face looks like. (Your thoughts might go back to what you felt in the exercise at the end of the previous chapter.) The same is true for pictures of you. But you, yourself, can never directly see your face. Spooky? You can witness your face in a picture or a mirror, but you can never actually see it directly. The import is that the one who is witnessing everything, can never be the witnessed. The subject cannot be the object. That is why the ultimate reality cannot be explained in usual terms.

WHAT WE ARE MOVING TOWARDS—WHY DO YOU WEEP, MY FRIEND?

The promise of Vedanta is that once we recognize our true nature, we go beyond sorrow, pain and suffering. The popular analogy of the dark room is a perfect example that demonstrates why we should even bother to set out in search of our true nature. Imagine a person sitting in a dark room on a sunny day, with the doors and windows shut. There is no other source of light in the room. The person is desperate to experience daylight, and is in great distress because they cannot see light. You must have felt by now that the solution is simple. The person should just open the door and step out to see sunlight. That is exactly what Vedanta is trying to suggest. When you are suffering, you need to open the doors and windows of your mind. Would you choose to continue suffering when you know there is a way out of it?

How can a vision of our true nature rid us of all suffering? It can be possible only if bliss is the truth of our existence. The entire purpose of Vedanta is to familiarize us with that blissful truth, expressed as *Sat Chit Ananda*—Existence, Consciousness, Bliss. In the Avadhuta Gita, a most immersive text, the poet explains our existence in multifarious ways. The entire book is suffused with the vision of that bliss that lies in the revelation of our true nature, and the fascinating poetic refrain is, 'Why do you weep, my friend?'[7] The poet reveals a vivid, blissful picture of the ultimate reality: 'free from passion, jealously, hatred and the rest […] that reality devoid of sufferings caused by physical, terrestrial, and supernatural agencies […] that Truth untouched by grief and misery of the world […] Existence-Knowledge-Bliss.'[8]

To unearth the bliss in your inner core, you need to understand what you are. Vedanta makes no secret of it. It says that you are Brahman, that ultimate reality, which is The One, projecting itself as many. At this stage, it is difficult to wrap our heads around this unreal-sounding concept. A little patience and the willingness to explore will help us arrive at an understanding of how that is true. As a reassurance, a special chapter in the Taittiriya Upanishad is aptly named 'Ananda Valli', meaning 'Chapter on Bliss'. It gives us an outline of the bliss that we are trying to achieve. The picture is unbelievably attractive.[9]

The Taittiriya Upanishad makes an interesting, lengthy calculation. It explains how the knowledge of that ultimate truth, our actual nature, can lead to unmatched bliss. It says, let's consider all the happiness possible for a person on this earth as one unit. That would include all the riches, knowledge, perfect health and all possible luxuries in this life. Then it starts multiplying this unit a hundredfold, taking into account all the happiness possible in other realms, till the unit has been multiplied by a hundred, all ten times. That much, the Upanishad says, is the joy one would experience if they get to know their real self. That is 10 raised to the power 20 of the original unit (which is all the happiness possible in this world). Incredible? Well, then that is worth striving for.[10]

WHAT IS TRUTH?

Since we are seeking what we call the ultimate truth of our existence, we need to be clear about what we mean when we use the word 'truth'. This could seem irrational to you, because in our everyday understanding, we think whatever we can see, feel, touch, smell or hear is the truth. In other words, whatever we can perceive with our mind and our sense organs is the truth.

However, that might not always be the case. Not all appearances in our world display the truth. The sunset is one such example. When we look at the glowing orange ball in the sky in the evening, nature is just playing a clever optical game with us. The sun has already gone below the horizon, but it appears to be right there, visible to us. The sky appears blue to us, but the air has no colour. The moon appears to shine at night, but it has no light of its own; it only reflects light from the sun. The leaf insect camouflages itself among leaves by looking like a leaf. Unless it moves, we cannot see that it is in fact an insect. There are countless examples in nature that demonstrate to us that what we perceive with our senses is not really the truth, not to mention the countless ideas that we carry in our brains. What we think to be true might be untrue for another person.

To prove something is true, there have to be specific parameters. Vedanta talks of the highest knowledge, therefore there must be clear defining parameters. In Vedanta, truth is something that can be modified neither in the three periods of time (past, present and future) nor in any dimension of space. What this means is that if something is true, it will not change in the past, present or future. If something is true, it will remain the same at any location in this world or, for that matter, in any place in the universe. Thus, truth has to be constant, unchanging, and independent of location in space.

Another criterion of truth in Vedanta is independent existence. If something is dependent on another for its existence, it is not truth. The classic example is that of the pot and clay. Consider an earthen pot made of clay. While the pot has a shape and a form, it is called a pot. However, the basic substance of that pot is clay. If the pot breaks, and loses its identity, the clay still remains the same. Thus, the clay is the truth of the pot. The existence of the pot is dependent on the clay. Hence, its existence is relative and comparatively false.

AVIDYA—THE HURDLE

Ignorance of the truth is the reason behind all our suffering and the suffering someone inflicts on others. The Upanishads have a technical term for this—*avidya*. Though its closest English translation is ignorance, avidya is a more broad-based term. The most important thing for us to know is that it is avidya—ignorance of our true nature—that keeps reality hidden from us, and that is the primary reason for our suffering. This ignorance is not like our ignorance of worldly things like not knowing a particular skill, or being unaware of things happening in some part of the world, for instance. Avidya is the *lack of knowledge of what we truly are*.

Since avidya is lack of knowledge, it is but logical that it can be cured by knowledge. Again, this knowledge is not the ordinary kind that we understand. At the highest level, this knowledge is the direct perception of the Absolute Truth of the universe—in other words, enlightenment. For more practical purposes, a glimpse of this knowledge can serve as the groundwork for solving the problems of our life. Once we know this, even theoretically, there will be a paradigm shift in the way we make choices, react to situations, and indicate preferences in life. In other words, even a glimpse of this reality is a doorway to bliss. This knowledge, however, is hidden from us because of avidya—the lack of true knowledge.

Avidya is an aspect of *maya*, which again is a complicated concept, as we will see later in the book. For now, suffice to say that maya is a power of the universe that creates illusory appearances in this world. It makes the unreal appear real. It projects things that appear to be true, but are actually false. In this way, maya has two roles: veiling and projecting. It veils reality and projects a world that appears to be real. So, our ignorance of our true nature is the working of maya, which hides our reality and projects this entire world as real to us.

Though maya and avidya are difficult to comprehend, a classic analogy explains these concepts effectively. The imagery of this analogy is used throughout Vedantic texts to elucidate the nature of this ignorance. If a rope is lying in your path, and somehow, due to the effect of shadow and light, it appears to be a snake from a distance, you might think it is a snake on the ground. If you believe that is a snake, for you, that is the reality of that moment. Hence, the snake is real to you.

However, when you actually realize that it was just a rope, the fear or anxiety that you might have experienced vanishes. What created that snake for you? The answer is your ignorance of the real nature of that rope. It was an error. Thus, error leads us to ignorance and that is how, when the ignorance about our true selves is removed, we see ourselves as we truly are. The Upanishads promise that even a little understanding of that truth is of great help in removing pain and suffering from our lives.

THE ROUTE

This part of our journey could be particularly difficult. Since avidya veils the truth, it has to be removed to unravel what lies behind it. Removing avidya is not as simple as it sounds. The problem lies not so much in the process, but with the conditioning of our minds. The knowledge of our true selves is extraordinary. But are we ready to receive it? What if you saw a snake instead of the rope and decided to remain fearful of that imaginary snake, even when someone tried to prove to you that the object was a rope? Unless you open yourself up to listening to that person and to giving them the opportunity to prove to you that it is a rope, you will remain in that state of illusory belief.

Consider another example. If a little child is led to a room where candies and chocolates are piled up on one table, and gold bars are piled up on another table, the child is most likely to choose candies and chocolates, with additional thought given to choosing between candies and chocolates. The interest in the gold would be non-existent. The choices most of us make are similar to this example. We tend to choose what gives us visible pleasure, and no matter how valuable introspection might be, we are not inclined towards it.

In order to remove pain and suffering from our lives, we need to identify what is valuable. How will that knowledge come to us? It can come only when our minds are conditioned to discern between what is of value and what isn't. You might ask, why is conditioning needed? Why can't we just have the answer?

Well, there are direct answers. The Upanishads and texts like the Bhagavad Gita give you straightforward answers. It is, like we mentioned, an open secret. This secret can be expressed in any of the *mahavakya*s or 'great sayings'— very short aphoristic statements that mention the highest reality. But if you read or hear any of these aphorisms, can you understand their import and what they are saying about your own life? Let's take this mahavakya in Sanskrit,

'*Aham Brahmasmi*,' from the Brihadaranyaka Upanishad, translated into English as 'I am Brahman.'[10] This is the entire truth of all existence and answers all questions. However, if someone is told just this, it is like telling the child in the aforementioned example that they should select gold over chocolates, without explaining to them the reasons for such a choice. Even if you explain the reasons to the child, the child needs to be convinced, and that can happen only if their mind has been conditioned to understand the concepts of money, wealth, value of gold, etc. Once the child knows the difference, they will make a better choice. In the case of the above mahavakya, one may ask what is meant by Brahman and what exactly is 'I'. Both these terms need an in-depth understanding of what they represent before the meaning of the sentence becomes clear.

This is why Vedantic scholars emphasize that this knowledge can be understood only by those minds that have been prepared to receive it. A four-fold qualification is mentioned as the ideal requirement for a person to understand the deepest truth. It is important to mention here that the bar is set quite high in the texts, since the aim is nothing less than enlightenment.*

However, we need not be discouraged. Many of us are not interested in spirituality or philosophy. Some of us do not want to go in that direction. Another set of people are contented with the way life is, except for the suffering. So, in short, all of us want a solution to the unpleasant things in life, but our desires and our methods may vary greatly.

---

*Check Chapter 8 and its Suggested Reading for more details.

If you are not zealously spiritual, you need not be disheartened. Even some percentage of the required conditioning of the mind is good enough to understand these concepts. Even if you are simply open to listening, that too is a great qualification. If you can consider and mull over some of the points mentioned, that is a great next step. And who knows, when you get a taste of the exquisite, you might develop a hunger to learn about the complete picture, and that would be the most beautiful turning point in your life. For now, let's help your mind understand the need to even look for the true nature of existence.

EXERCISE

The purpose of this exercise is to help you see your preferences and the conditioning of your mind as a whole, as the larger picture. Though the requirement has been expressed in a few words, you might want to spend some time at this stage, mulling over the questions.

1. Imagine, if you had to wish for one thing, after which you would not want anything else in the world, what would that be?

Write it down. It could be an object, a situation, an event, a possession, a relationship, or anything physical or subtle.

_____
_____
_____
_____

Now explain to yourself why that thing is your ultimate desire. How would it make you feel? Would you feel fulfilled, or supremely happy, or satisfied, for instance?

2. Explain to yourself how the presence of that thing will affect all other areas of your life. This might take some time. If you wish for an object, explain how it would affect your relationships, as an example. If you wish for a relationship, think about whether it could change equations in your career, as another example. Or, if it is fame and money you wish for, would it make you the healthiest person going around? Whatever you wished for would be just one thing in your life. Try to imagine how having just that one thing would change everything about your life. Write down the thoughts that come to your mind as answers to these questions.

When you have done both the exercises, read your answers and give yourself time to reflect upon the answers before proceeding to the next chapter.

Please note that you might or might not find clear answers to these questions. That does not matter. What matters is that you become aware of how your mind thinks, and desires things in this world. The purpose is to help you gain clarity about your own thought process.

8

THE METHOD AND THE ROUTE

The exercise at the end of the previous chapter might have brought to your notice the vicious cycle of our desires. Our desires are not satiated with one thing. The pleasure that comes from the best of experiences is limited in time. You can be delighted about a skydiving experience, for instance, but for how long? Maybe a few days? After that, you would be looking for another experience to give you a feeling of happiness. Or, when you finally buy something that you have been planning for a long time, you will feel happy. Even that feeling of joy will subside in a few days. Even if we get what we desire the most, it is not the solution to the other problems that keep cropping up in our lives. That one thing that we wish for does not make all the other areas of our lives perfect. As a result, we are always trapped in an endless cycle of wishing and working to fulfil those wishes. This too is the working of avidya, the antithesis of true knowledge. It entraps us in an endless cycle of desiring things that will give us happiness, and of striving to fulfil those desires. Since all our energy is directed towards fulfilling those aspirations, we are unable to focus single-mindedly on the truth.

The first step toward removing avidya is the conditioning of our minds, as we have seen. In the previously discussed example of the child, if the child had understood that choosing gold over chocolates would ensure a lifetime supply of chocolate instead of just a few pieces, they would make an informed choice.

Here is a heartwarming claim: if you have come this far in the workbook, you already have one primary qualification for moving ahead on this path—curiosity. If you are willing to reflect deeply on the points mentioned so far, that is an added advantage. Equipped with these two traits, let us explore the kind of conditioning of the mind that is required to get a glimpse of that which is the solution to all problems.

THE PREREQUISITES (See Suggested Reading*)

As mentioned in Vedantic texts, there are four prerequisites or preliminary qualifications for being a seeker of the ultimate truth. There are two levels at which we can understand each of these prerequisites—the ultimate spiritual level and the practical level. In other words, if you are seeking enlightenment, these qualifications need to be greatly refined and continuously practised. However, for most of us who are looking for a solution to suffering, even some effort to acquire these qualifications is helpful.

The first qualification is *viveka* or the ability to discern. In the Vedantic context, it means the ability to differentiate between the real and the unreal, what is absolute truth and what is conditional truth. At our level of practicality, let us say that this is the ability to differentiate between the important and the unimportant. When we are suffering, it is important to find a solution, while it is unimportant to wallow in self-pity. It is important to understand that suffering is temporary, but it is unimportant to focus on how miserable the suffering is making you. This discernment, this ability can be cultivated by everyday practices. For instance, when someone is being mean to you, it is important to give a response, but it is not important to harbour deep resentment within you.

The second qualifications is *vairagya*, or dispassion. At the highest level, this means dispassion for all temporal things of this world, including matter, mind and desires. As beginners, we can begin cultivating vairagya by understanding that everything in the world has a temporary existence. For us, this would be an understanding and acceptance that nothing stays forever—neither misery nor happiness. The cultivation of this dispassion does not mean that we have to become uninterested in life and its matters. Rather, dispassion is a tool to recognize that something better than the impermanent exists, and *that* is what we should have passion for. It is a way to condition our minds to understand that if we lose something, it is okay. Sadness too is temporary.

The third requirement is not a single quality but six treasures, collectively called *shamadishtasampatti*. These subtle 'treasures' are *shama*, *dama*, *uparati*, *titiksha*, *shraddha* and *samadhan*. While the technical terms might seem intimidating, these are simple faculties of the mind, the kind that we might use in learning anything new—for instance, a new subject at school.

Shama is control of the mind. When you have to learn a new concept, say driving, you need to condition your mind to pay attention to the instructions. For that, you need to control the mind from flitting elsewhere. Dama means control of the senses, or the organs of the body. If during driving lessons, you get hungry, wouldn't you control that urge and complete the lesson? That is dama.

Uparati is a higher state of shama and dama, where the control becomes spontaneous; you no longer have to make a huge effort for it. It can be exemplified in a situation where you have to drive back from work every day, and say it is a long drive. You have trained your mind sufficiently to focus on the driving (shama), and to control other urges that you might have like hunger or thirst, or the idea of folding your sleeves while your hand is on the steering wheel (dama). When the control becomes spontaneous for you, that is uparati.

The next of these six treasures is titiksha, or fortitude. In the spiritual context, it refers to a patient endurance of all sorrows and pain. For us, it can mean that whenever a problem arises, we can take a deep breath and tell ourselves that no problem will stay forever, so this too shall pass. We can train our minds to be patient while actively trying to find a solution to the problem. The fifth of the six treasures is called shraddha. The word is generally understood to mean faith, but this faith is of a more practical kind. It is the kind of faith you have in a source of knowledge, say a book or a teacher teaching you a particular subject. When you learn to drive, you have faith in the instructor that whatever they are teaching must be correct. That is shraddha. It never means blind faith; it only means that you need to trust the source of knowledge enough to help it help you.

The sixth treasure is called samadhan. For a spiritual

seeker, this means a deep concentration on the objective, to know the ultimate truth of the universe and this existence. For us in the practical domain, it means focus. You will not be able to learn anything unless you focus your mind, be it driving or basic cooking. It is, therefore, ideal to concentrate on the matter being taught to derive the maximum benefit from it.

The final requirement, the fourth of the four-fold qualifications, is *mumukshuta*—an intense desire to be free, a deep longing for solutions to problems. For the religiously inclined, it is the cry of the heart, calling out to God, to show them a way. For the spiritual, it is the yearning to understand the ultimate truth, to solve all the mysteries of existence. For the person of science, it is a powerful conviction that there are answers to the riddles of the universe, which can be found through intensely focused effort. For the practical person, it is the burning desire to find answers to the problems of life in order to set oneself free from pain and suffering.

The four prerequisites, as we have seen, are attainable, although at first glance they might seem lofty and distant. To summarize, to start walking on the path of understanding the mysteries behind pain and suffering in the world, we need to condition our minds. This conditioning includes establishing a distinction between the important and the unimportant and a dispassion for the unimportant. It further includes a certain disciplining of the mind required to learn anything new, including self-control, patience, and faith in the ideas being communicated. An intense longing to know the truth is the most important requirement. Unless you have the desire, you will not be able to even start your journey. If you maintain that passion, you will reach your destination.

A UNIQUE APPROACH

Vichara

Once the prerequisites are cultivated to at least some degree in the individual, the mind yearns for the truth. It is worthwhile to mention here that the way of Vedanta is a bit different from other spiritual paths. For instance, the path of devotion, common to all theistic religions, requires one to have belief in God or a higher power. The focus is on proving the existence of God and how the world relates to that supreme power. Non-theistic religions focus on the power of nature or impersonal forces that guide our fate. The path of yoga, on the other hand, lays stress on control of the mind to realize the supreme.

However, the way of Vedanta is quite different. It is the way of *vichara*, or enquiry. The word 'enquiry' here does not only mean a simple question or a simple problem statement. It is much more than just a thought process. It is a deep dive into the depths of our being. This enquiry starts with our direct experiences of everyday life, and matures into a more profound understanding of ourselves and the world around us. This method of analysis is suffused with logic at every step. It never asks you to take a leap of faith. The Upanishads and the explanatory texts are replete with counterarguments too. Most strikingly, Vedanta asks you to believe in its claims only when you feel them for yourself. In other words, unless it feels real to you, you need to keep questioning and exploring.

But why an enquiry? The reason sounds simple but has a profound meaning. Since the cause of our suffering is avidya, the lack of true knowledge, it is imperative that the only thing that removes that suffering is knowledge. As Adi Shankaracharya says in *Aparokshanubhuti*, 'Knowledge is not brought about by any other means than Vichara, just as an object is nowhere perceived (seen) without the help of light.'[1] That light is the knowledge that we are seeking.

The Three Steps

This vichara is not just curiosity, but an entire system of studying, scrutinizing and applying. That is why there are three well-defined steps in this process. The first one is called *shravana*. It literally means 'hearing', but has a broader meaning—reading the texts, or listening to a teacher, or any means by which you are introduced to the concept. The idea is to familiarize you with the ideas expounded in Vedantic texts. This listening has to be active, just like there is a difference between passively hearing the sound of something and listening to it with attention.

The next step is *manana*, which means thinking about and reflecting on what you have heard, read or learnt. This stage is important because you need to give good thought to the concept you have been introduced to. That is why at this stage you are expected to have many questions. Doubts and queries are an integral part of the process, and are actively encouraged to help you go deeper into the meaning and relevance of the teaching.

The third step is where the learning becomes real for you. This is called *nididhyasana*—applying and checking the ideas for yourself. This is the stage when you test for yourself what is being claimed in the texts. While doing this, you must keep in mind that if you have the prerequisite qualifications, at least to some degree, along with the desire to know the truth, this becomes easier for you. Even if you have a vague idea of what is being talked about, you still gain a lot. The very act of trying to apply the teachings is a huge step away from ignorance. At the highest level, nididhyasana is the stage at which a person comes face to face with the deepest secrets of the cosmos, and hence with the true nature of their own existence.

SUBJECT AND OBJECT

A crucial aspect of Vedantic analysis is understanding the terms 'subject' and 'object'. In the philosophical context, these terms are useful tools that help us realize the difference between reality and non-reality. To explain this at a basic level, if you perceive anything, you are the subject and that which you perceive is the object. For instance, if you smell flowers, the fragrance is the object and you are the subject. If you see the book in your hands, the book is the object and you are the subject. Even mental states like sadness or happiness are experienced by you. Therefore, you are the subject and the emotions are the objects. The same holds true for your memories and thoughts. In short, whatever you can perceive is an object to you.

Here is an important point: the object and the subject can never be the same entity. To perceive something, you have to be different from it. In other words, the subject can never be the object of perception. Herein, it is important to introduce a term—the Self (with a capital S). It is the real self which we are trying to reach, our innermost reality. It is different from the self which we refer to as our identity, this self of the mind–body–ego complex. Hence, it becomes essential to constantly differentiate between the Self and the non-Self. The Self can never be an object of perception because it is the one witnessing everything else, including this self of the mind–body–ego complex.

These concepts might sound esoteric, but some understanding of these is crucial in our journey ahead. The analysis of the discrimination between the Self and the not-Self requires us to keep an eye on this important discernment. To summarize, anything which is an object of perception to you, which you can see, feel, hear, touch or perceive in any way, is an object, and hence not the real you.

NETI NETI

Since this enquiry is into the deepest mystery of the universe, this endeavour is nothing like our usual efforts. This reality is beyond all that is known and all that is unknown, and is not immediately perceivable to us. Throughout the centuries, it has been acknowledged that it is difficult to explain this approach through language, or music, or science, or any known medium of human expression. The Katha Upanishad pronounces, 'It cannot be attained through speech, nor through mind, nor through eye.'[2]

It is due to this difficulty that a novel approach was used by ancient scholars to explain this truth. This method is known as *neti neti* which, when translated into English, means 'not this, not this'. It is a method of negation, or a series of negations. The reason is simple: when something cannot be expressed through an affirmative statement, we can try to explain it by considering what it is not. When we consider all possibilities, and each is negated, at the end of all negations lies only the truth. Gaudapada explains this in his *Mandukya Karika*, 'Since by taking the help of incomprehensibility (of Brahman) as a reason, all that was explained earlier (as a means for the knowledge of Brahman) is negated by the text, "This Self is that which has been described 'Not this, not this'", therefore the birthless Self becomes self-revealed.'[3]

Let's now go to the next steps to see how we can gradually understand this and get the answers to everything that troubles our mind. Before that, let us try to practise conditioning our minds to receive that knowledge.

EXERCISES

The following exercises are to develop the faculties of the mind in a way that the mind is conditioned to receive the truth. That is a gradual process. Therefore, these need to be tried repeatedly, as you go along your routine day, or any time a situation arises. Remember, the purpose is the conditioning of the mind, and this will take time. The conditioning needs to be maintained with consistent practice. You may want to set a routine to practise these exercises, or you may want to come back now and then and work on them. Let's do these for the first time right now. (These exercises are independent of each other and can be done in any order. Also, they need not be done together.)

a) Try to think of your entire life, including the past and the future life to come. Include the events in your life that you consider important, your actions or reactions to them, your thoughts and emotions. Focus especially on how you reacted to the situations. Take each event or situation one by one and see yourself responding in the way that you did. You may write these down in detail, or you may write short hints, as some memories can be vague.

_____
_____
_____
_____
_____
_____
_____
_____
_____

Once you have done this for the past, shift your attention to your future, or your visualization of your future. Think of what you desire, what you fear, or whatever thoughts come to your mind when you think of the future. Note these down. You may make a list of the things you want and those that you want to avoid.

_____
_____
_____
_____
_____
_____
_____
_____

When you have given enough thought to the past and the future, take all of it together and see your life as a whole.

Now, carefully try to separate the important from the unimportant. Write down the things that you feel you should not have done. Write down the things that you feel you must start doing in the present. Also list the things that you think you should do in the future. While doing this, apply the method of seeing yourself as another person from a distance. When you see your life as a whole, what are the things that you would want to add and what are the things that you would want to remove from your life?

To further practise this, as you move through every day in your life, try to consciously differentiate between the things that would make you feel better in the long run, and those that will lead to future dissatisfaction. You may modify this exercise to discriminate between the important and the unimportant in different situations in your life—career, relationships, personal choices and the like. Now, you have begun to practise viveka to some degree.

b) Think of an object that you cherished in the past. It should be an object which you do not have now. It could be anything you had—a gadget, some piece of clothing or jewellery, or a book. Now revisit the memories of the days when it meant a lot to you. Take, for example, your first mobile phone. In your memory, recall the feeling that you had, wanting to take care of it, being curious about its features, all that you can remember. Recall how, in those moments, the thought of losing that object could have made you anxious or worried. Relive those moments. Write down your thought process around that object, including your reactions in relation to it. How did you feel when you lost it or when you stopped using it?

_____
_____
_____
_____
_____
_____
_____
_____
_____
_____

Now bring your thoughts to the present. Think of a number of things that you possess right now. There could be possessions that you greatly cherish—your phone, a book, a gadget, a gift, your car, clothes, or maybe a piece of art. Consider losing those things one day. Write down how you would feel when that happens.

_____
_____
_____
_____
_____
_____
_____
_____
_____

Here is an important thing. At first, you might be disturbed, but practise telling yourself that even if you lose an object, you will be fine, just like you were with so many other objects that have come into your life and are not there anymore. Repeat this through the days, whenever you can. That is the beginning of the practice of vairagya.

c) Practising the six treasures, shamadishtasampatti, will be a multifaceted exercise. Here are some things that you can do.
   1. Visualize a theoretical scenario where someone has annoyed you or angered you in some way. You may also recall an unpleasant incident that has happened to you. In your mind, picture yourself responding calmly to the person. Here's how to do it. Take a deep

breath. Tell yourself that you are going to stay calm, no matter how obnoxious the other person might sound. Imagine yourself giving a firm but controlled response. Write down the scene and see how that makes you feel. You may want to write this down in the form of a dialogue or as a continuous narration. You may also want to write just a part of it—your responses. That is fine. The important thing is to see yourself in your mind maintaining your composure even when the other person is being rude or mean to you. It could be like a movie script you are writing for the hero. You are the cool hero in this case.

_____
_____
_____
_____
_____
_____
_____
_____
_____
_____
_____
_____
_____
_____
_____

If such a situation actually arises in life, recall the script that you have written and practise giving calm responses.

2. Imagine your favourite food item is in front of you, served, ready to be eaten. Visualize yourself not being tempted by it. Imagine leaving it on the table and going back to doing other things for at least an hour. That would definitely not be easy. But practise it in your mind, and write down the sequence of events. Then, when you are ready, try to do it some time in real life. Keep your favourite food in front of your eyes, and tell yourself you will not have it for the time period you have decided. It could be a few minutes to begin with.

_____
_____
_____
_____
_____
_____
_____
_____
_____
_____
_____
_____
_____

3. The following will be a hard one, and you might not want to do it at first, but slowly bring yourself to visualize this. Recall any situation in the past when you were hurt or sad. Write down how you

felt in those moments. What were your thoughts? For instance, did you feel anger or hatred towards a person in that situation? Were there any feelings of self-pity or helplessness?

_____
_____
_____
_____
_____
_____
_____
_____
_____
_____
_____
_____

Now, bring your thoughts to the present. You might notice that the intensity of the hurt or sadness has decreased. The force with which those thoughts affected you in the past is much reduced now. Write down how you feel about it in the present. You will notice that while you might still be sad, it is quite different from the way you felt earlier.

_____
_____
_____

Tell yourself that when a painful situation arises in the future, you will remember that it will heal with time. That it will pass. Practise patience in similar circumstances in your thoughts, and when the situation arises, apply that in life. Tell yourself this mantra: 'This will pass.' You are practising patient forbearance. Please remember that it is not helplessness. You are practising empowering yourself with control.

4. At least for two minutes a day, try to practise focusing. If you are already involved in practices such as meditation or similar exercises, it is an advantage. However, since most of us are not, let us take a simple way to practise it. You may write or you may do it orally, if you want. This is a more practical form of meditation. The objective is to focus on one thing at a time.

Think of anything that you really like. It could be

a place, a dress, an event, or any physical object. Think only about that object. Start describing it, but without comparing it with other things. Every thought and sentence should be about the place or object in focus. Your thoughts will flit, but you have to come back to describing the object under consideration. You are practising how to focus. You can try to do this any time of the day, or you can fix a time, such as just before you go to sleep.

___

d) This one will require deeper introspection. Write down the questions that haunt you most in life. It could be the fear of death, fear of serious illness, separation, grief, or any aspect that makes you question the very purpose of life. Thinking on these lines is a little difficult, because most of the time we tend to avoid such thoughts. But avoiding such thoughts is not the solution either.

Now, when you have recalled the questions that you have, imagine there is someone who can give you answers to these questions. Surely, someone must have answers to these deep questions. If you are religious or spiritual, you can concentrate on God or the Ultimate Reality. That Supreme Being, if you believe in one, can definitely address your apprehensions.

If you are not religious or spiritual, you can imagine a fictitious entity in your mind. It could be a scientist, an astronomer, a philosopher, or maybe a vague entity that can help you find the solutions to your fears.

Now try to visualize your chosen entity in your mind and share your fears and apprehensions with them. This might not be a one-time activity. As you go through your daily routine, let your mind experience a longing to approach that entity to urge it to answer the questions for you. Let your desire to find the solutions deepen, till it begins to feel like a true longing. You will find yourself moving towards mumukshuta. You may write your visualizations in the space below.

_____
_____
_____
_____
_____
_____
_____
_____
_____

9

YOU ARE NOT THE BODY

By now, we have progressed quite well up the ladder, and we are at a stage where we will begin to differentiate between the Self and the non-Self. In other words, from these steps onwards, we will get a clearer picture by separating the real from the unreal. Let's start with the most obvious—our physical identity.

When we think of ourselves, we invariably identify with our bodies a certain appearance, a certain race, and certain differentiating features. Even our official documents contain a picture of us which is supposed to be an identification of the person that we are. We mention recognizing marks such as a mole on the nose, our height, the colour of our hair and our body weight as added descriptions. These bodies of ours and the faces that we have serve as our primary identities in life.

For those of us who think a little deeper, we see ourselves as a mind in a body, which we call our inner self. We think that it is not just our bodies, but our thoughts, our words and our intentions that define us better. At an intellectual level, we understand that we are more than our appearance.

The 'truer' us, we think, is our personality, which is a combination of our physical appearance, our thoughts and our actions. The religious and spiritual ones among us might think that there is a soul in this body and we might have an idea that the soul is a deeper dimension of us.

Here is the problem. All of the above assumptions, in one way or the other, take the body as the ultimate definition of a person. Even the soul is supposed to be *in* the body, although invisible and hence unprovable. This directly implies that we exist as long as this body exists. Do we cease to exist when the body dies?

HOLD YOUR BREATH!

In stark contrast to our common conceptions, Vedanta makes a stunning claim: you are not your body, nor the contents of your body. You are not even an individual soul. You are much greater than that. You are never born and you will never die. You are eternal. You are ever-free of sorrow and suffering. There never was a time when you did not exist and there never will be a time when you will cease to be. You are existence itself. You are none other than the ultimate reality of the universe. You are Sat, Chit, Ananda—Existence, Consciousness, Bliss.

The above-mentioned ideas might be earthshaking for most of us. What is being suggested here is so counterintuitive that even a lifetime might be insufficient to grasp the scope of this idea. These suggestions are mind-boggling to say the least, like a bolt from the blue that shatters the ideas gathered over a lifetime. They might seem like fiction, or might have the ring of impractical philosophy. Yet, the only grand project of the entire corpus of Vedantic literature is to prove to you that this is the only truth. There are multifarious arguments in favour of this assertion. The trio that forms the basis of Vedantic study, the Upanishads, the Bhagavad Gita and the Brahma Sutras, all tirelessly attempt to bring home this idea.

To simplify it a little, now is the time to introduce the technical name for the ultimate reality, our ultimate truth that we are striving to reach. That ultimate reality is expressed in one word—Brahman. It is pronounced 'brahm' in Sanskrit and 'brahaman' in English, and is entirely different from the caste tag Brahmin, and also from the name of the deity Brahma. Brahman is also referred to as *Atman* or even *Purusha,* though there are subtle subjective conditions for using these terms. Here, you might be naturally inclined to ask if Brahman is the same as God. Though the terms 'God' and 'Brahman' are sometimes used as synonyms, the former term implies the unmanifest appearing as the manifest. Mentions of God or any synonymous terms in the Upanishads refer to a personalized concept of the abstract Absolute Reality.

So, does Vedanta claim that the ultimate reality is God, or the other names with which we address the concept of God? The answer to this is neither in the affirmative, nor in the negative. The answer is the most jaw-dropping claim yet—that the ultimate reality is no one else but you, and that the real you is none other than the Absolute, call it God if you may. You are that reality. That 'real' you is the answer to all your questions; you are *that* even when you are in pain and suffering. The commonly understood concept of God is *Ishvara* in Vedanta, and it is nothing other than the Absolute appearing as an entity with its own power of manifestation. Just as you exist, and your neighbour exists, Ishvara exists wherever the manifestation is needed.

If these concepts are confusing as of now, that is expected. To resolve this confusion, these terms need to be qualified by a detailed and deeper understanding. What do we mean when we say 'you'? The terms 'I' or 'you' are approached through this systematic enquiry that leads us to a direct, undiluted realization. For now, this much can be qualified that 'I' here does not refer to our personality aggregate. The nature of that ultimate truth is so subtle that it can be fully understood only by direct revelation. In other words, unless you perceive it first-hand, you would not fully understand what it means. That is a tall order, but there is a consolation for us. If we even get a basic intellectual understanding of these concepts, that alone is sufficient to solve our obsession with suffering.

The nature of our quest is fantastical and subtle. The truth we are searching for is expressed in the Kena Upanishad thus: 'The eye does not go there, nor speech, nor mind. We do not know (Brahman to be such and such) hence we are not aware of any process of instructing about It.'[1] Then it goes on to add, 'That (Brahman) is surely different from the known; and again, It is above the unknown...'[2]

Since what we are trying to find is inexplicably subtle, the most effective way to do it is through the process of elimination. Let's see what we are not, and arrive at the truth through a series of negations. A magnificent array of evidence is presented before us to prove that we are not just the body. Vedantic arguments are remarkable because they operate on logic. You are not asked to believe in anything that you cannot see or experience for yourself. Rather, you are expected to come up with doubts and questions, which have been answered somewhere or the other in the vast but profound body of Upanishadic understanding. In fact, the method is strikingly similar to that of scientific enquiry. Both science and Vedanta draw information from real experience, rely on observable data, and need an absolute open-mindedness. Thus, keeping our minds open, let's explore the various layers of this stunning revelation.

Unlike the other chapters in this book, this chapter has two exercises—one mentioned below and another at the end of the chapter. The midway exercise in this chapter will be useful to you in evaluating your current state before moving on to the actual method of neti neti.

EXERCISE 1: THE IDEA OF YOU

Before we dive deep into the detailed explanation that Vedanta gives us, we must be clear about where we are standing. More importantly, we must be able to 'see' for ourselves where we are right now. Otherwise, the explanations would not be absorbed to full effect. Take the following exercise and stay with it for some time, till the idea becomes clear. Then move on to the next section of this chapter.

Sit calmly for a few minutes in a comfortable position. Avoid distractions. Close your eyes and say 'I'. Then say 'This is me.' Give yourself some time to think it over. Keep your eyes closed and think of 'I' and 'me', and say 'Here am I.' Stay with the thought. If you visualize yourself as your appearance, as how you appear to other people, bring your thought to your own mind. Here is the important part: concentrate on the idea of 'I' and see where it is. Can you locate it inside or outside your body? Can you feel that 'I'? Write down any ideas that come to your mind. Do not worry if this seems abstract. Just note down whatever thoughts come to you. Focus on where you feel that 'I' is; where you perceive your true locus to be.

_____
_____
_____
_____
_____
_____
_____
_____
_____

ONE OR MANY?

If the above exercise seemed difficult, do not lose heart. We all would have only a vague, confusing idea of where this 'I' is. That is how human perception is, and this is where Vedanta will guide us. Keeping the previous exercise in mind, let's start with the core analysis of what we are, or rather, what we are not. Let's begin with the physical appearance of the body.

If you look at any part of your body, say your hand, for instance, what do you think? You probably say to yourself, 'This is my hand.' The same is true for your feet, your nose, your knees, your neck or any part of your body. Now think.

Can any of these parts individually claim to be you? In other words, your hand alone is not you. The idea of you as a physical entity is a collection of all the parts of the body. However, here is the stunning thing. When you say 'I', it seems to be one and not many. You feel that you are one entity, not many entities that have come together; but the body is defined by the many parts it is made of. You are one, but the body is composed of many, hence the body cannot be you.

Also look at the statements 'this is my hand' or 'this is my body'. We refer to our physical selves using these terms. These clearly show possession. We feel that we are owners of this body of ours. This means you are separate from your body. You can possess only that from which you are separate. You cannot possess yourself. You are the subject and the body you are perceiving is the object. This again proves that you are something more than the physical body.

In *Aparokshanubhuti*, Adi Shankaracharya says, 'How strange it is that a person ignorantly rests contented with the idea that he is the body, while he knows it as something belonging to him (and therefore apart from him) even as a person who sees a pot (knows it as apart from him)!'[3] He adds, in relation to the many parts of the body, 'The Supreme known as "I" is but one, whereas the gross bodies are many. So how can this body be Purusha?'[4] Thus, the physical body is an aggregate of parts, but you are one.

INTERNAL OR EXTERNAL?

Again, when you draw your attention to the idea of 'I', you feel you are somewhere in the body, right? But where exactly are you—in the blood, in the head, in the fingers, or elsewhere? Even your internal organs are objects of perception to you. For example, you think of your heart as 'my heart'. The same is true for all the constituent parts of your body. Thus, whatever you are, you definitely *possess* the internal parts of your body.

Just like the external organs, all the internal organs come together to make this body. None of those parts individually defines you. Your brain, or your heart, or your blood are not the complete you. Your body is composed of around thirty trillion cells (which is thirty followed by twelve zeroes). Each of your organs is made of billions of cells, which are further made up of numerous subcellular components. These components are further made up of atoms and molecules which, again, are made of subatomic particles and fields. There is a whole multitude of components that make up your body, internally and externally. Yet, you feel you are one. You are a singular entity, but your body is an aggregate of components. So how can your body be your complete reality?

SENTIENT OR INSENTIENT?

Now that you are beginning to feel that you are internal to your body and all the components of your physical body can be perceived by you, focus your attention to another fact. You are conscious, sentient, aware. However, none of your organs, internal or external, are conscious by themselves. You feel aware, but does your hand by itself feel aware? This might sound vague, but think for a moment: aren't you the one making the hand work? Or, for that matter, aren't you the one who is making the heart beat? This clearly determines that you are separate from your body, because the body is insentient, but you experience sentience.

FORMLESS OR WITH FORM?

When you think of 'me', 'mine' or 'I', do you feel yourself to be of a specific shape or form? You might say that you are in the shape of this body. Just for a moment, think of yourself as different from your body. Now, do you feel you are abstract? Vedantic texts continuously draw our attention to this idea that we are formless, yet somehow, we identify with this form that we call the body. (See Suggested Reading*)

CHANGING OR UNCHANGING?

Change is the very nature of the body. There are perpetual changes going on in every cell of our body. Biochemical processes, transfer of energy, and the metabolism are just a few examples of the constant flux at the micro level inside our organ systems. Even the blood in your body is not the same all the time because each red blood cell is active up to only around 120 days, after which it is replaced with a new cell. Your hair and your nails keep growing. Hence, you do not have the nails that you had at birth. The cells on your skin are continuously shedding. In fact, the top layer of your skin is replenished every thirty days.

In short, your body replaces billions of cells in different organs every day. So, if you are holding on to the idea of this body being the complete you, you would have to keep pace with the rapid rate at which the body changes continuously.

At another level, think of how the body ceaselessly changes even in appearance. You were born as an infant one day. Then you were a baby, then a toddler, and after your childhood, you became a teenager and then an adult. This same body will grow old. Yet, the person in the body of the baby is the same person that is in the body that you have right now. The body changes, but you, the awareness behind all those changes, remain constant. So, how can you be the body?

The above five arguments are meant to bring home the idea that we are much more than mere bodies. The concept may or may not sink in right now, but to get a fair idea of what this is about, let's practise some exercises.

EXERCISE 2

a) Have you seen a picture of yourself from when you were a baby? Try to imagine yourself in that body. Give it some time. Then think of yourself a little older and see yourself in that body. Let the image float in your mind. Then, picture yourself in your mind as you were five years ago. In each of these visualizations, recall the details of your physical appearance, your hair, your height, and other features.

_____
_____
_____
_____
_____

Then bring your attention to the present. Think of the body you have right now. Is it the same as it was in all those earlier stages? Do you feel you were the same person in all those stages of your life? Write down whatever thoughts come to your mind when you are doing these visualization exercises. Here, writing is secondary. The important thing is to use your imagination to consider the idea that you have been the same, but your body has been constantly undergoing changes.

b) Recall a time when you got a mark or a bruise or a wound on a part of your body. How did it look? Do you remember the appearance of the bruise? How did it look when it started healing after some time? Look at the same part of your body now. Is it the same as when it was hurt? Write down what you think about this.

_____
_____
_____
_____
_____
_____
_____
_____
_____

c) For this exercise, read the instructions, make a mental note, and then sit in a quiet place and visualize. Close your eyes and think of how you see your physical body. Are you aware of your limbs, for instance? Now, are you aware that some processes are going on inside your body, whether or not you can define them?

Now, you need to pay close attention because this is a paradigm shift. Consider this fact: you are observing this body—its internal as well as external aspects. Let this sink in. Repeat to yourself: 'I am observing my body because I am aware of it.' Here is the greatest shift: since you are aware of your body, you are the observer, not the observed. Think of this for some time. Think of it as you go through your day. You may want to write down how you feel about this.

_____
_____
_____
_____

10

YOU ARE NOT THE MIND

'Virtue and vice, pleasure and pain, are of the mind, not of you.'[1] This embodies one of the deepest secrets for practical living, which, if understood properly, can lead to freedom from all pain and suffering. The great sage Ashtavakra pronounces this to his worthy disciple Sage-King Janaka in one of the greatest Vedantic texts, the Ashtavakra Gita, also known as the Ashtavakra Samhita.

Just think of one thing that has provided you happiness in the last few days. Let's say it was a particular food item that you ate. The taste, the texture and the aroma made you feel really happy. Yet, this thing that we call happiness did not exist in the food itself. The food does not have any ingredient called happiness. It was your mind that created the feeling of joy. The same is true for sadness too. This idea that you are different from your mind, however, will take some time to be understood because we usually know ourselves as our minds.

Though it may take some time for you to get used to the ideas discussed in the previous chapter, when you perceive yourself as different from your body, the feeling will be of reassurance. You know that pain and disease is of the body, but you are clearly something separate from it. You perceive the pain, but it is the body that suffers, not you. You might feel the pain in the body as a thought in your mind.

However, if you are told that the subtle entity inside you that you think of as your mind is not you either, it would be hard to digest. Even more than our bodies, we identify ourselves with our minds—our deepest thoughts, our likes and dislikes, our passions, and our memories. But Vedanta says that even your mind is not your complete reality.

Yet, we experience suffering in the mind. When there is pain in the body, the pain is converted into suffering in the mind. You feel that you are sad, anxious or pained, all in the mind. Hence, you suffer both in the body and mind. What if you could prevent the physical pain from converting into suffering in the mind? That is the next step that we are moving towards. After claiming that you are not the body, Vedanta is taking us towards another astounding claim—that you are not even your mind. In your daily experiences, you might often feel that the truer you is somewhere in the physical body. You might have felt yourself to be a vague, shapeless entity located in your head or brain, or maybe somewhere in your chest area. Most of the time, you probably think of yourself as the mind.

Here, we must differentiate between a couple of fundamental concepts. First, the mind is different from the brain. The brain is a physical organ that carries on the biochemical processes through which the entire body functions. It generates sensations, feelings and responses. Therefore, though it is a physical object, the brain creates subtle things like thoughts and emotions. When we speak of the mind, however, we refer to only subtle things like thoughts, memories and emotions. A collective of these subtle attributes is what we generally call the mind.

Another differentiation is to be made between the mind and the soul. But even before that, the word 'soul' has to be qualified. The English word 'soul' is not a very accurate translation of the word 'Atman'. Atman is synonymous with Brahman, the ultimate reality, which is all-encompassing and not individual. There is a minor difference in usage, as when we use the word 'Brahman', we are looking from the standpoint of the ultimate reality, but when we use the word 'Atman', we are starting from the standpoint of the individual. The two words, however, mean the same thing. The word 'soul', on the other hand, refers to individual entities that give sentience to bodies. Souls are parts of the universal soul or super soul, identified with individual bodies. In short, Atman is a more appropriate description in this context because it is all-pervasive, immutable, and beyond all perception. You cannot know the Atman or Brahman through any medium. It can be perceived only directly.

Coming to the difference between mind and Atman, the mind is just a small aspect of Atman. It is one of the attributes of the latter. Atman is eternal, while the mind is ephemeral. Atman is all-encompassing but the mind is localized to one individual. This distinction between the two is necessary because in common understanding, the mind is often confused with the soul or the sentient entity in the body.

To come back to the mind, it can be scary if you are suddenly told that you are not your mind. It does not mean that you will become an insentient object, or that you will lose control of your body. It also does not mean that something else is controlling your mind. Just think of it as a computer system. There is a processing unit that analyses data and basically carries out all the processes in the computer. Those processes lead to the display on the screen, but there are a number of unseen processes going on behind the scenes. When you go to sleep, the mind shuts down, but it does not vanish; just like when you shut down your computer, the data is still there, but the computer is not actively working.

Similarly, in dreamless sleep, under anaesthesia, or in a coma, the mind is not active, but the person is still there. The mind will start functioning again when one comes out of these conditions. The mind is essentially different from the real you. This is the next step towards understanding our true nature and getting to the root of all our suffering. The Upanishads and related literature present several arguments to prove to us that we are much more than just our minds. (See Suggested Reading*)

THE MIND—AN INSTRUMENT

Let's look at the mind from a different perspective which will make it easier for us to relate to what the mind actually is. If we talk in terms of Vedantic philosophy, the technical term that is the equivalent of the English word 'mind' is *antahkarna*. The word 'antahkarna' literally means 'inner instrument' and is sometimes also called the inner organ, though it is not considered an organ in the physical sense. It is interesting to note that the mind is spoken of as an instrument with which we interact with the world. If you notice the subtle difference, this means that the mind is a helpful tool, but it is not the entirety of our existence. That means you must be more than your mind.

The antahkarna is supposed to have four aspects, classified according to their functions. The first of these is *manas* or that aspect of the mind which observes, perceives and works with the sense organs and motor functions of the body to enable our interaction with the world. The second function is called *buddhi*, which is the intellect. It is through our buddhi that we make decisions and exercise discernment between good and bad, desirable and undesirable. This part enables us to differentiate truth from falsehood.

The third aspect is *chit*, the seat of memories and thought impressions. It is through the functioning of this aspect that we remember or forget things. It is also a place where impressions are stored from our various experiences. The fourth function of the mind is called *ahamkara*. While the literal translation of ahamkara is 'ego', it means the identifying part of our personality. This is the feeling of 'I-ness'. It is the faculty of the mind that helps you articulate your own identity as 'I' or 'me'. As you can see, these functions are not watertight compartments. They work in coordination. As a collective, they constitute the instrument called the mind. What is noteworthy here is that the mind is not a physical entity, yet we are aware of the mind as we are of our bodies.

THE MIND CHANGES IN TIME

As we go through life, the body undergoes continuous changes, and along with the body, the mind also changes. A toddler's mind is different from that of a teenager. A young person's mind has different inclinations from those of an old person. A baby might feel joyful on hearing the sound of a musical toy, but when it grows into an adult, the same sound could be annoying. A child might be scared of dogs, but as they grow older, the fear could vanish.

You perceived the world differently when you were a baby, but as you grew older, your likes, dislikes and thoughts transformed. Various factors account for these changes. They can take place because you gain knowledge, process that knowledge, and form a belief system in your mind.

Here is something important for you to note. While your mind keeps changing with age, *you* remain constant. It was the same you who had the mind of a baby, and the same you that has this mind now which is processing the words written in this book. Thus, *you* are constant, but the mind changes with time. Hence, the mind cannot be your complete reality.

THE MIND CHANGES IN SPACE

Let's examine another perspective now. Even if you ignore the development of the mind through time, let's consider a relatively stable period of time, say a single day. Your mind behaves differently in different places. You could be calm at home, and stressed at work. You could be happy talking to a certain person but, minutes later, you could dislike the company of another person. You could feel motivated sitting at your desk, but disillusioned when in another space. You could be happy about going to certain places you love visiting, like a favourite restaurant, or be upset when forced to go to a place you do not like visiting.

In addition, the mind is fickle, sometimes experiencing different emotions within a short period of time. You might have experienced situations where conflicting thoughts flit through your mind at the same time. There are times when you are unsure of which option is the right one, like in deciding what to buy. Thus, your mind is constantly in a state of flux; but again, it is important to note that it is the same *you* who is experiencing these different states of the mind. Anything that changes cannot be the ultimate reality. The absolute truth in Vedanta does not change with time and space. *You* remain constant, but your mind changes, so you are something more than your mind.

THE MIND IS AN OBJECT OF AWARENESS

In the above-mentioned situations, you must have noticed how you are aware of your mind in different states. It is the same you who is aware of the annoyance and of your mind being joyful, for instance. In other words, you can clearly 'see' your mind in various states. Since you can see your mind, how can you be the mind? As mentioned earlier, anything that is an object of your awareness cannot be your awareness. In other words, anything that you can perceive, see, hear, touch, feel or comprehend has to be different from you. Hence, once again, it seems clear that you are not just your mind; your mind is just a part of you.

POSSESSION

A subtle point emerges from the above discussion. You are the owner of your mind; it is not the other way around. Your identity is more than the mind. You, the real you, are observing the mind and its various functions. Which means you are beyond the mind. You can also describe how your mind experienced great happiness during a certain event, or how it experienced deep sadness when something else happened. Also observe the language in which you address the mind. You might say 'My mind is calm now' or 'I am feeling anxious'. The fact that you use such pronouns indicates that the mind is something separate from you. You are not it; you have it; you experience it. Hence, the mind is clearly an object of perception to you.

ONE AND MANY

Through all the aforementioned descriptions, you must have figured out that you are a unity while the experiences are varied. You are one, and the states of mind are many. You are the witness to those different states of the mind—happiness, sadness, stress and relaxation, among others. You also experience the mind performing different functions. You are aware of your mind generating emotions. You are also aware of the memories that your mind stores and recalls when needed. When you use your intellect to solve problems, you are a witness to your mind performing those functions. You also notice the ego in your mind—the identity of 'I'. Thus, you are one, but the functions of the mind are many. You cannot say that you are only your intellect, or only your memories, for instance.

A GIANT LEAP

Since most of your perception of suffering arises in the mind, when you successfully see your mind as different from you, you have taken a giant leap. This might take some time to sink in, but once you grasp this idea, you have found the master key to bliss and peace. Your mind is like a unity, and in this unity arise different waves of emotions and thoughts, and into it again they fall back. Your mind remains just that—your mind, which you possess and experience.

This is beautifully expressed in the *Avadhuta Gita*, in which the poet Dattatreya sings: 'Why should I care about the waves of the mind? They appear and disappear like bubbles in water.'[2] The imagery is striking and immediately liberating. Imagine a body of water in which waves are formed, but the waves merge back into the water. Bubbles might arise, but the bubbles too settle down into the same water. Your mind is like that. Any emotion that arises in your mind dissipates after some time. The duration might be long or short, but the emotion definitely subsides and can be recalled again only through memory.

The same analogy is again beautifully presented in Yoga Vasishtha Sarah. The seer Vasishtha, while teaching Vedanta to his disciple Rama, says, 'Like fitful ripples on the surface of the tranquil ocean, this restless mind is created out of that widespread, extremely tranquil, changeless supreme Self.'[3] This is a notch above the previously mentioned verse. Here, the mind is described as arising out of you, and you have been compared to the tranquil, changeless ocean. Your absolute nature is that of tranquillity and the mind is created like ripples out of that peaceful state. If you get the meaning of this symbolism, you will immediately see a resolution for all your pain and suffering. The Yoga Vasishtha Sarah further explains how the restless mind is created, even though its original state is peaceful. It says, 'To accept that which is agreeable and to renounce absolutely that which is disagreeable is the very nature of the mind. Know this to be bondage alone and nothing other than this.'[4]

Thus, we have reached a heartwarming assurance—it is possible for all beings to go back to that state of undisturbed tranquillity, the state where there is no suffering, no misery, just absolute peace, even though external events of all kinds keep happening to the person. The 'Advaita Prakarana' (Chapter on Non-Duality) of the *Mandukya Karika* points out: 'When the mind does not become lost nor is scattered, when it is motionless and does not appear in the form of objects, then it becomes Brahman… That highest Bliss is located in one's own Self.'[5]

EXERCISES

a) Sit down in a quiet place. Be comfortable and read through this exercise. When you start practising, you may close your eyes, or you may imagine the situations below with open eyes if that works for you.

 Recall any time from your childhood that you remember in some detail. It could be a time when you were hurt, or when you were extremely happy. It could be a time of anxiety before an exam, or the feeling of freedom when school got over for the day. Pick any one event. Try to recall the sequence in as much detail as you can, including your actions, your words, and your thoughts. If you do not remember many details, that is fine. Try to recall what you felt like in those moments. Try to think of how your mind worked at that time. Stay in that time in the past and 'see' yourself in that mental state—what made you angry, what were the things that scared or annoyed you, what made you feel safe or happy—in short, all the emotions and feelings the situation invoked. Then write down everything that you recalled. While writing down, focus on describing your state of mind and not on the external events that happened.

_____

_____

_____

_____

_____

_____

_____

_____

_____

_____

_____

b) Now, think of a time at least ten years after the event that you have just described. Recall a particular incident, an event from that time. It could be a sad one, a happy one or even a boring one. First visualize in your mind what took place and then recall how you were thinking at that time. Try to fill in as many details as possible—your reactions, emotions or thoughts about that event.

Now, take the first and the second exercises together, and write a comparative account of how your mind behaved on these two different occasions separated by ten years.

114 ■ THE TRUE HAPPINESS WORKBOOK

_____
_____
_____
_____

c) Recall a recent incident, a conversation or anything that affected you in a positive or negative way. As you close your eyes, see yourself having the thoughts, emotions and reactions that you had towards that event. Try to write down the thoughts that had passed through your mind.

_____
_____
_____
_____
_____
_____
_____
_____
_____
_____
_____
_____

d) Answer the following questions after thinking about the previous exercises:
Were you able to see (imagine/visualize) yourself in different states of mind—happy, sad, angry, frustrated, satisfied, etc.?

Look at any object around you, say a pen or a book. Are you different from the book?

Why are you different from it? (Here, you may answer by saying that you are different from the object because you are aware of its existence.)

Were you aware of your thoughts in each of the incidents described above; as in, were you aware that 'I am thinking…' or 'I am feeling this…'?

So, you were aware of your mind and the different thoughts arising in your mind? For example, could you recall having thoughts like 'I felt really frustrated at that time' or 'I thought I had behaved in a mature way'? Hence, do you see that you are different from your mind?

Note: Even if you do not have specific answers to the aforementioned questions, keep trying in your routine activities to 'see' the mind and its thoughts. You can do this while going about your daily life, or if you like, you can sit down and do this with concentration.

As you progress, keep reminding yourself that you are the witness to your mind. You 'see' your mind in different states. When you experience that revelation, you will have taken a huge step towards empowering yourself. You will be able to understand that you are more powerful than your mind.

11

THE SUBTLE BODY

As we have seen by now, neither the body nor the mind expresses our complete truth. Practically speaking, we do not experience ourselves as only the mind or only the body. So, what is this mind–body complex, and is there something other than this that defines what we are? Vedanta presents an interesting classification of the different factors that make up our personality. While the classification might not be of direct relevance to you in your day-to-day living, having an idea of this makes it easier to understand how we function as individuals and how different layers of our being interact with our environment. That helps us find the locus of our suffering.

This concept of personality is a comprehensive picture that encompasses everything from the physical body to the subtle mind. It is interesting that both the mind and the body are matter to Vedanta, one being subtle matter and the other being physical matter. It would be worthwhile to mention here that our true nature is beyond even this personality. So, what is it that cannot be covered even by this comprehensive range of all that is visible and invisible? The path to answer this is our continuing negation, an analysis of what we are not. The next concept in this sequence is called the subtle body.

The subtle body is imagined like layers of matter covering the truth (See Suggested Reading*). This matter is not matter as we understand in the ordinary sense; it includes subtle aspects like the mind too. These layers are called sheaths, the term indicating that each layer is tightly wrapped around its inner layers. You may imagine it like a fabric roll firmly enveloping a centre. The centre is the truth, your original nature, hidden by these layers. That core is the deepest secret to be unearthed, but to see it, we have to remove those layers one by one. To do that, we have to start with the outermost layer, one that is most clearly visible to us.

This outermost layer is called the *annamaya kosha*. It is nothing other than our physical body. Since each part of our body, big or minute, is formed directly or indirectly by food, this sheath is also called the food sheath. In the previous chapters, we have seen that this body is not our entire reality; hence, after having removed this layer of misunderstanding, we see the next sheath.

The next layer is known as the *pranamaya kosha*. In other words, all life processes that go on in a living person are included in this layer. This is why it is the layer of life forces, and is also known as the energy layer. It includes breathing, all the chemical processes in the organs, all the biochemical processes within the cells of the organs, the enzymes, the hormones, and various other processes that sustain life in a living body. This is the layer where disease arises, since any illness is due to some malfunction of the life forces. This is also the level of our existence at which we feel hunger, thirst, tiredness, and such indicators that are related to keeping the body healthy. Since all these are internal processes of the body, they are not our entire truth either.

The next layer is called the *manomaya kosha*. It includes all the functions of the mind, along with our sense organs, as we have seen in detail in the previous chapter. You must have felt you are something beyond even this sheath. But this is just the third layer.

The next layer is the *vigyanamaya kosha*. This is the layer of your existence where knowledge and reason are located. This layer helps you understand, analyse and interpret. Since you are aware of your analyses, thoughts, reasoning and knowledge, even this layer is not the real you.

Beyond the sheath of knowledge lies the *anandamaya kosha*. This is the seat of bliss, which is of the nature of your absolute reality, but even this is not the real you. The absolute reality is even beyond this one. At the same time, this layer is the closest to the truth, and derives its blissful state from the real you. This is also called the causal body, and is different from both the subtle and the gross bodies. The word 'gross' refers to the physical body. The subtle body thus includes the mind, the life forces and the intellect—three *kosha*s that we have discussed above.

The anandamaya kosha is like a reserve of bliss. We feel flashes of this bliss in various experiences in life, like in moments when we see something beautiful, or when a certain sight generates a feeling of awe in us. The moments of happiness that we experience due to sublime things like music, a work of art, or the discovery of something, reflect this bliss. In this layer, the ideas of ego and identity are absent.

Does this sound fantastical to you? Well, we all experience this blissful state every night when we are in deep sleep. Deep sleep is different from the sleep in which we have dreams. In this state, our everyday experiences, thoughts, memories, emotions and physical behaviours remain in a latent state, a kind of seed state. Our minds are not actively functioning at this time, though the contents of the mind are there, as if quietened for some time and asked to sit still. They come back as soon as we wake up.

Yet, during the deep sleep state, we experience only nothingness. It is important to note that it is still an experience for us, though at that time, we are not aware of having that experience. But when we wake up, we can recall that we were in deep sleep where we had no dreams. For those of you who are sceptical about this, you may take the help of devices like smart watches that can monitor the exact amount of time you were in the dreamless sleep state, called the non-rapid eye movement (NREM) sleep. The point is that this experience of nothingness is the sheath of bliss, the layer closest to our real nature. Yet, even this is not our innermost reality. It is called the causal state as our waking and dream states lie in a dormant or seed form in this state. Since this state too is an object of our awareness, this is not the real us. Hence, our search for our deepest truth has to go a step further, and for that, a little more conditioning is needed, as we will see going forward.

For now, let's consolidate the observations we have already made—all the subtle aspects and all the physical aspects of our bodies are matter. To simplify, whatever you are aware of can be taken as matter. That includes the physical body, the subtle body and the causal body.

Whatever is matter cannot be the real you because matter is transient, limited and an object of your awareness. The real you is the observer of all these states.

If you look carefully, by this time you would have figured out that all your problems, your sorrows and your suffering lie in the layers of the subtle body. The layers cover the real you, and thus, suffering cannot touch you—it stays in these layers only. Here, we have to make a careful distinction.

THE POWERFUL ANALYSIS OF THE THREE STATES

By now, you have seen that you are not just your mind or your body, or even your subtle body. To supplement this understanding, we can draw upon the method of the three states, as mentioned in the Mandukya Upanishad, and explained in detail by Gaudapada.

Gaudapada's seminal work *Mandukya Karika*—treatises on the Mandukya Upanishad— presents a powerful line of argumentation based totally on our experiential learning from everyday observations. (See Suggested Reading*) The four chapters of the karika are powerful expositions of the nature of reality. This work is unmatched for its profound perspective that uses the highest philosophy to reveal the strongest arguments in favour of the non-dual nature of reality. However, for our purpose here, let's focus only on its basic elements. Those alone are enough to help us differentiate between the real and the unreal. Its basic premise is that any person goes through three experiences in life that occur cyclically—waking, dreaming and deep sleep. Profound analyses follow to show how a person experiences and registers these states.

One powerful, thought-provoking fact is presented here. We all know that dreams are not real. They are gone when we wake up, and we instantly realize that whatever we were seeing in our dreams was false. That is true of both pleasant dreams and nightmares. But consider a subtle fact here. While we dream, we think it is real. Don't we? We cry in the dream, we laugh, we run, we are hungry, we sense hot and cold, we smell fragrances, we are chased, we miss trains or flights, we are anxious, we are relieved. We see animals, birds, furniture, buildings, vehicles, and all sorts of objects. Our dreams take place in different environments like a home, an examination hall, or outdoors. Sometimes the setting is familiar and sometimes it isn't. All that seems real to us when we are dreaming.

Now here is a suggestion. What if your current life is also a dream? When you wake up, you might find that whatever you are experiencing right now was only a dream. You will instantly object: there is a long period when you go to sleep every day and wake up and that is how life goes on. Consider this: even in a dream, days, weeks, years pass by and everything seems absolutely real. You might argue that you currently feel your pain and your anxiety. But that is true of your dream too. Sometimes, the dream is extremely distressing, but that feeling is gone after waking up. You might say that you can taste, feel, hear and speak in this life, but, again, you do all that in the dream too.

Now for a stunning statement from Gaudapada: 'As the dream-objects are unreal in a dream, so also, because of that very reason, the objects in the waking state are unreal.'[1] Is that a suggestion that this life is not real? That this life is false appearance? To answer this, we need to qualify the words 'false' and 'real'. When you see a snake in the rope (ref. one of the previously discussed examples), the snake is real for the time you think it to be a snake, but it is false when you recognize it is a rope. Similarly, this life is real as long as we identify it to be everything. Once we see the core of it, it will appear to be false. Having said that, our experiences of this life, body and mind are real while they last, but when we see that the rope was the reality, and the snake was an illusion, we see the reality behind the false appearance.

Gaudapada presents arguments that are hard to refute, but since they belong more in the domain of serious philosophy, let's consider a simpler part of them. Just as all experiences and objects in our dream have a beginning and an end, similarly, all that we experience in our lives begins and ends. Anything that is not constant through time and space is *not* the ultimate truth. It only has a temporary reality, like the snake in the rope. The snake is real only while the illusion lasts.

In addition, the objects of the dream depend on the dreamer's mind, and anything that borrows its existence from something else is false. Similarly, the existence of objects in our waking state, subtle and physical, mind and matter, depends on us perceiving them. The real you is the witness of these objects. Without your awareness, the objects do not exist for you. This too is borrowed existence, hence unreal.

The difference, says Gaudapada, is in the organs of perception. What that means is that our physical senses, in conjunction with the mind, make us aware of the objects in the waking state, while the impressions in the mind and our memories make us aware of the objects in the dream state.

The consciousness behind both is the same. It is important to note that objects are perceived in both the dreaming and waking states, and that whatever is perceived by you is separate from you.

The other state is sleep. Deep sleep or dreamless sleep is when we are not conscious of our body or mind, or even of the thought that we exist. It is, like we have seen earlier, a state where the mind and all thought are temporarily suspended. This too is experienced by you, though during the time of the experience, there is no such thought as 'I am experiencing blankness in deep sleep.' Yet, when you wake up, you can recall being in deep sleep, sleep where you did not have any dreams.

These suggestions might seem uncanny to you, even unnerving. If that is the case, just think of the last disturbing dream you had, and the relief you experienced on waking up and realizing that all that was just a falsity. Waking up from this life is also the end of all suffering; it is nothing other than the knowledge of what we truly are. It is the relief you will feel when you remove an illusion, when you realize that the 'object' in your path is not a snake but just a rope. At the same time, you must keep in mind that while the illusion lasts, you will try your best to keep yourself safe from the snake.

The important thing that underlies all the points mentioned above is that it is the same you, the same awareness, which experiences these three states. You are the witness of these states, hence you are separate from these. At the same time, these experiences occur in you, hence they are projected only from you. The word 'you' here means the real you, the witness of all these, the Self, the reality that we are slowly striving to completely understand.

Gaudapada uses the term *turiya*, a word whose literal meaning is 'the fourth'.[2] The term is essential because in addition to the three obvious states, a fourth has to be mentioned, even though the fourth is the substratum of these three. Turiya is actually the *only* reality, and the three states arise and subside in it. It is the same as consciousness, Brahman, Self, or Atman.

The classic Vedantic example used to illustrate this is that of the gold jewellery (See Suggested Reading*). Consider three pieces of jewellery—a bangle, a necklace and a ring, all made of gold. These three objects have different appearances, their utility is different, hence the three have different functions. Though their forms and functions are different, the substratum is the same metal—gold. If the three ornaments were melted in a jewellery shop, they would lose their form and only the gold would remain. Similarly, turiya is the true, fundamental reality, and the waking, dreaming and deep-sleep states all arise and fade in it. This is just a glimpse into your true nature that holds within it all your experiences.

With these breathtaking ideas, we get a sense of all that we are not. We have negated the reality of the body and mind, and all waking and sleeping experiences. Now, we move towards affirmation. Since we know that the rope is not a snake, just like we know that the water in the mirage is not water, we can now take another step up towards getting a glimpse of what lies beyond these negations. Gaudapada nudges our intellect with this question, 'If all objects in both the states be unreal, who apprehends these objects and who indeed is their creator?'[3] To arrive at the revelation, let's ground ourselves first in what we have seen so far.

EXERCISE

You might do this exercise while sitting or standing. Just make sure you can concentrate on the requirement of this exercise. Take any book (or a notebook) and place it in front of you.
Relax, keep blinking normally, and look at the book.
What is looking at the book? Is it your eyes?

_____
_____

Are you aware of your eyes looking at the book?

_____
_____

What is aware of your eyes looking at the book?

_____
_____

Is it your mind?

_____
_____

Are you aware of your mind registering the thought that your eyes are looking at the book?

_____
_____

Can you 'see' your mind being aware of this chain of thoughts?

_____
_____

Think of this one carefully—what do you think is giving power to your mind to register all these thoughts?

That one, the one that is aware of the mind, of the eyes and also of the book, is the real you. Now close your eyes and feel the real you looking at the mind that is driving your experience. Open your eyes and say, 'I am aware of the thoughts in my mind. I am the witness of those thoughts. I am beyond the body, beyond the mind and beyond the thoughts. I am the reality behind all these.'

You may repeat the exercise with another object or with the same one. You may also repeat the exercise as many times as you want till you grasp what is it in you that is aware of everything, including your mind and its thoughts.

That real you, witnessing the five layers of your mind–body, witnessing the myriad experiences that you have, has been revealed after removing the layers one by one. Let's brace ourselves to see its magnificent luminosity.

12

YOU ARE THE WITNESS

Here you are, close to the summit of the ladder. Let's recapitulate the steps that have brought you here: The experience of pain is real and should not be negated, but you do not have to suffer because of your pain. Pain and suffering are not you; you are much greater than these experiences. Hence the question—what is it that *is you*? When you climbed up the ladder to know what *you* are not, you found that you are not your body or the zillion processes going on in it. You are not even your mind or your composite personality. You are not even an aggregate of all these put together. After negating everything, what remains?

You are none of these, yet *you are*.

The one that is aware of all those negations, *you are*.

The one that is aware of what you thought was you, *you are*.

The one that is aware of you being aware of that observation, *you are*.

Even if you are totally ignorant of everything, still, *you are*.

You are. Read that again.

You cannot say 'I'm not.' You can negate all that you

experience, or see, or perceive, but you cannot negate that *you exist*, that it is *in* your awareness that you experience all that appears to you as the universe. Even in states such as coma, deep sleep, unconsciousness, you do not comprehend anything. Yet *you are*.

You exist. You are none of your parts or their aggregate, yet you lend existence to all these. You are existence itself. You are the consciousness in which all these experiences occur, because without consciousness, none of this is possible. You might want to pause here. You might want to give this some thought: is awareness of anything possible without consciousness? Approaching the question from all possible angles will lead you to the same answer. You cannot be aware of anything material or non-material without consciousness.

That one, the real you, beyond all the layers of being that carry pain and sorrow, is bliss itself, untouched by either sorrow or happiness. It is pure, not in the sense of being clean or unblemished, but in the sense of being the most fundamental, unmoulded and unshaped—the very basis of everything. You are pure existence, pure consciousness, pure bliss. The supreme reality according to Vedanta is Brahman—Sat, Chit, Ananda. That fundamental existence, you are. You are Brahman. That is your truth. It is you who are the witness of the body, the mind, the subtle body and all the processes associated with them.

This is the point in the workbook where either your intellect will experience a flash of understanding, or you may become very apprehensive. Your instinct will be to either delve deeper into that understanding, or to outright refute it by looking at the world. It is reassuring that both paths will lead you to the same bliss. There is no wrong path. The only important thing is to keep going.

Understandably, these revelations might be shocking for you. You might experience fear at the thought of not being able to comprehend yourself. Do not try to comprehend yourself. You are the one in which all comprehension rests. You are untouched by it. You are even beyond all kinds of fear. The apprehension or fear is being felt by your mind; you are only witnessing your mind doing that.

Yet, if the thought of you being different from all that you can see, hear, smell, taste, touch or think of sounds unsettling, just think of your dreams. When you are experiencing a dream, you are untouched by whatever happens in the dream—be it burning your hand in a fire, or being chased by a monster, or falling into a gorge. The same is true for your pleasant experiences. You might have felt the touch of a trophy after winning a competition in your dream, but actually you never touched anything of the sort. You were sleeping. Says Gaudapada, 'As in a dream the mind vibrates, as though having dual aspects, so in the waking state the mind vibrates as though with two facets.'[1]

Similarly, this entire life, in the body and mind, sleeping or dreaming, all the things that you experience are appearances in the reality that you are. These appearances are transitory. They change. *You* remain. To make this idea more understandable, let's explore this further with the help of a Vedantic story.

THE TENTH MAN STORY

This well-known story is about ten men who cross a river by wading through the water. When they reach the other bank, they want to ensure that all of them have crossed safely. One of them starts counting, and takes into account the nine others, but forgets to count himself. The group is concerned. Another man volunteers and starts counting. He too counts everyone else but himself. This goes on till every man has tried counting. Each one forgets to count himself. They start wailing in grief, thinking that one of them has drowned.

Then a stranger, who has been watching them from a distance and realized the mistake they have been making, volunteers to help out. He counts from one to nine and turning to the tenth man says, 'You are the tenth.' The men realize the mistake they have been making and feel relieved.

Likewise, you usually count yourself as your body, your senses, your mind, your intellect, your personality, and the various components of the layers of your being, as we have seen, but you forget to count yourself, who is witnessing all those layers. The stranger who can help you see yourself is none other than the knowledge of your true self. It was only your ignorance of your true self that resulted in your suffering, just as forgetting to count themselves was the cause of the ten men's suffering in the story.

WHAT YOU ARE LIKE

'It is known to him to whom It is unknown; he does not know to whom It is known. It is unknown to those who know well, and known to those who do not know.'[2] This cryptic verse from the Kena Upanishad, referring to your true nature, seems to present an insurmountable problem. It is not, however, just a clever play of words. It is the truth.

Let us recall an earlier example. Imagine yourself

looking at your face in the mirror. It is only because of the reflection in the mirror that you know that you have that face. You can never see your own face directly. Any part of your face—the eyes, the skin, the nose or the lips—cannot show your face to you. It is only through the reflection in the mirror that you can understand what your face looks like. The example is not perfect, but the point has been made. Your true nature, the consciousness behind everything, cannot be comprehended by any of your senses, or the body or the mind. But you know that you exist, which is why the consciousness is known to you, though it is unknown to you in the empirical sense. That is why, in the above verse, it is stated that if someone says that they *know* consciousness, they have not understood it at all.

The one that is the witness of everything cannot be the object of any inference. It is itself the perceiver, hence it cannot be perceived. Something that cannot be perceived cannot be described. That is the difficulty of describing the true nature of your innermost self. The vast body of Vedantic literature tirelessly tries to achieve this goal of finding a way to describe the nature of the Self. The Self is the highest reality, the answer to all queries, the substratum of everything in this universe. Multifarious attempts have been made to describe what you truly are, but none can do justice because this reality cannot be approached through the senses, or the mind, or the body, or the intellect. It cannot be described in language.

It can only be known directly. As you might have felt in some previous exercises, that *something* within you is aware of even your mind having thoughts—that is the Self. The predicament is expressed like this in the Kena Upanishad: 'The eye does not go there, nor speech, nor mind. We do not know Brahman to be such and such; hence, we are not aware of any process of instructing about it... That is surely different from the known; and again, It is above the unknown.'[3] The Upanishad goes further to describe that that which is known through each state of consciousness, through every experience, is nothing other than Brahman, or your consciousness, or the real you. You do not have to go anywhere, or understand anything other than your own experience, to understand your true nature. You only have to recognize the witness consciousness behind every experience of yours.

There are numerous such poetic expressions to describe the Self, but a particularly beautiful and comprehensive description exists in the Mandukya Upanishad. It is said to encompass the entire message of our quest for our true nature. It says:

> ...that which is not conscious of the internal world, nor conscious of the external world, nor conscious of both the worlds, nor a mass of consciousness, nor conscious, nor unconscious; which is unseen, beyond empirical dealings, beyond the grasp (of the organs of action), uninferable, unthinkable, indescribable; whose valid proof consists in the single belief in the Self; in which all phenomena cease; and which is unchanging, auspicious, and non-dual. That is the Self, and That is to be known.[4]

There is an interesting pattern in this verse. The first half is negation and the second half is affirmation. Yet, in the affirmative statements, the nature of the Self cannot be actually described; it can only be known through direct experience. This portrayal of your true nature is grandiose, subtle and glorious, yet it might be hard for you to reconcile it with the fact that you live in this world and you experience it with your body, mind and senses.

Where, then, is the role of this hidden consciousness? Apparently, the mind–body is doing everything. And if consciousness is the substratum of everything, why is it hidden and so difficult to perceive? It might look splendid in poetic descriptions but is it really there in us and in every entity? To solve this great mystery, a subtle bridge needs to be created between that ultimate reality and the physical you, this mind–body complex of yours. For that, we must move to a most complex yet fascinating part of our journey. But before that, let us calm our minds to visualize our basic reality—the sat chit ananda that we are.

EXERCISES

a) Sit down in a comfortable position. Read through this exercise and then close your eyes.
Say 'I am.'
Think of the location of the feeling of 'I' in your body.
When you say 'I', do you think you are in the upper or lower part of your body?

_____

_____

Then come to your hands and arms. Can you say that the 'I' is somewhere in your arms or hands?

_____

_____

After that, shift your focus to your stomach. Can you say 'I am in the stomach?'

Shift your attention to your chest area. Do you feel the 'I' somewhere there?

Focus now on the head. When you say 'This is me,' is it somewhere in your head?

Most likely, you would have found that the feeling of 'I' exists in the head, behind the eyes, or probably in the chest. When you perceive that, hold on to the thought and feel the 'I' or 'me' there. Stay with it for some time. Now comes the most important part. Do not rush through it. When you are ready, think of who is watching that 'I'.

Here is the secret:

That one, who is watching that 'I' is the real you.[5]

It is the witness, it is the consciousness, it is Brahman, it is you. That real you was witnessing this entire thought process of yours—when you felt you were not really in the legs or the stomach, when you thought that you were probably in the chest. That 'I' that you were seeing in the head was the ego-identity, the individual identity of this personality, but the one who was *seeing* that ego-identity, is the real you.

b) Sit in a comfortable posture in a quiet place after reading the following exercise:

Recall what is the greatest trouble in your life right now. It could be a physical problem or something that is troubling you mentally. Now, using the experience of the previous exercise, locate the witness that you are. Watch your trouble and your thoughts from that position. Identify the gap between the location of the trouble and the real you. You will find that the real you, the witness, is untouched by whatever pain there is in the body or mind. When you are able to identify the distance, look at your trouble objectively. Tell yourself that the trouble is temporary. It will subside. You, the real you, will remain unscathed by it. If you feel like, you can write about it.

_____
_____
_____
_____
_____
_____
_____
_____
_____
_____

c) Imagine you are wearing a VR (Virtual Reality) headset—a device through which you can see a simulation on a screen just next to your eyes, and you get auditory inputs in your ears. Together with the sound and the sight, you get the false impression of being in another world, because the headset blocks your vision and the sound of your real surroundings. The visuals are designed in a way so that as you move your body or tilt your head, the field of vision changes. As a result, it appears as if you are in another setting, almost in another world.

Now, imagine you are wearing a VR headset that has you perched on top of a fifty-storey building. There is a Burma bridge made entirely of thin rope that you have to cross to reach the top of the other building. Imagine yourself walking step by step on that bridge swinging precariously that high up in the air. Since your sensory inputs tell you that you are on that bridge, while stepping forward, you would take all precautions and feel a rush of fear when you slip.

Now, write down the two perspectives from which you have experienced this. One, what you would have felt while in the game. Your impulses would have acted according to the dangers in the game—the slipping of the foot, the fear of heights and such other conditions. Write down how you acted according to the sensory inputs you got, for instance the slipping of the foot. How did that make you feel?

_____
_____
_____
_____
_____
_____
_____
_____

___

___

___

The second viewpoint would be of your actual situation. When you were playing that game, in reality you were in a room, and not in the game, acting as if you were a real person in a real setting in the game. When you think from this perspective, and you look at yourself acting in the game, what are the thoughts that come to your mind?

___

___

___

___

___

___

___

___

___

___

To further extend the purpose of this exercise, at any time during your routine when you find yourself feeling bad or miserable, look at yourself as if you were looking at your avatar in the game. You are always witnessing your body and mind reacting and behaving in a certain way. In that state of distress, 'witness' yourself feeling miserable, and communicate that this will pass, and you will be fine, that it is just a temporary state.

13

THE MYSTERY OF THE WITNESS

By this stage in our journey, you have identified yourself with your true reality, the consciousness that is the witness of everything. You are the witness consciousness to which the mind, the body and the world appear. Now arises a fundamental problem, one that transforms the entire argument into a surreal concept. If you are this witness, Brahman, the ultimate reality, then what is this mind, body and world that you perceive? You are the witness, you see the body grow older, you see diseases come and go, you see emotions rise and fall in the mind. You see phenomena happening in the world—the sun rises, rain falls, plants grow. You *see* all of this.

Most intriguingly, there are other people who are as conscious as you. If you are the witness of those people and even other creatures, then is the same true for each of them too? Is each person or organism an individual witness to everything else? Does this mean that the ultimate truth is unique to each person and that each person is a separate witness? That would be quite a crowd. That would also mean that for every person, there is a subjective revelation, hence a rose that appears red to you might appear green to another person. You think water is wet, but what if someone feels that water is dry to touch? Such bizarre conclusions would be possible based on the assumption that each consciousness is separate from the other. The argument is a self-defeating one, because anything that is the ultimate truth of existence, has to be one. The approaches to it might be many, but the truth itself must be one. The Rig Veda declares: 'To what is One, sages give many a title...'[1] This idea that the Truth is one, but the wise call it by various names, was one that Swami Vivekananda reiterated at many occasions, including in his speech at the Parliament of the World's Religions held in 1893.

To address this predicament, the masters of Vedanta have presented comprehensive descriptions and systematic reasoning to show just one thing—there is no diversity, no duality when it comes to the ultimate reality. It is one reality that appears as all this—the diversity and the myriad experiences associated with it. That reality is Brahman and that reality is you. You are That. That might sound hard to imagine right now, but let us see how this spectacular truth unfolds and is vouched for by the most brilliant philosophers through the ages.

NON-DUALITY—THE HIGHEST REALITY

The problem before us is this: how can you, the consciousness, be the one reality of all this diversity that you perceive? The diversity is mind-boggling. You see other people, objects, animals, stars, air, water, innumerable material things. Other than what you can see in your immediate surroundings, the world is inhabited by approximately 435,000 species of plants and around 8.7 million species of animals. Of the latter, only 1.2 million are properly known and the rest are being explored. When it comes to our species itself, no less than an upwards of 8 billion humans, each individual is different from the other. Besides, there are countless inanimate objects that inhabit not just the earth but also the entire universe. And it is not just the numbers. It is also the scale. Our earth itself is smaller than a grain of sand in the vast expanse of the cosmos. When you start gaining knowledge, how much of it can you absorb? Even if you study your entire life, there is just a miniscule fraction that you will understand in depth. You cannot know about every part of everything in this universe.

Just as you start getting comfortable with the idea that you are the witness consciousness witnessing the plurality of the world, Vedanta tells you that this entire universe is nothing other than you. The scenario has shifted dramatically. If you are witnessing the universe, who creates and manages things in the universe? When you are told that you are the universe, the thought is overwhelming. At this point in our journey, explanations seem to get abstruse, and philosophy seems to take precedence over logic. However, we had started with the understanding that we will use logical interpretations that will be demonstrated by our everyday experiences to arrive at the truth.

So here we are, taking the help of the most extensive research possible that humankind has witnessed through the centuries. On the surface, this research looks different from the scientific research that we are used to in contemporary times. Yet, the essence, the approach and the zeal remain the same. This research, carried out in the laboratories of the mind and of life, requires the right conditions for the experiment to go well. We have seen earlier in the book what those conditions are. An indispensable ingredient is the belief that truth is approachable, a key driving factor that also propels any scientific quest to startling discoveries.

In this quest, this highest reality has been perceived and revealed through several spiritual masters down the ages. It has been recorded in various Vedantic texts, not as something that can be experienced, but as the one reality beyond which nothing remains to be understood. Not just sages, but ordinary people too have reached that understanding. When one has even a rudimentary knowledge of that highest non-duality, all suffering ceases. Only bliss remains. Since that one reality is difficult to describe, Vedanta uses analogies, imagery and stories to help us understand the path to reach that ultimate truth.

THE DREAM PARADIGM

One of these is the dream paradigm. Let us take an example. Imagine yourself having a dream where you are getting late for an exam. In the dream, you are trying to have breakfast, but the sandwich keeps slipping from your hands onto your plate. You notice an ant crawling towards your plate. The scene changes abruptly, as it often happens in a dream, and you are on a bus. Time is ticking but it appears that the bus will not be able to reach on time. The bus is full of people and the person sitting next to you happens to be from your past and looks exactly like she did many years ago. She engages you in a conversation and you fear that while talking to her, you will forget what you prepared for your exam. The frustration and fear within you are rising. You start sweating. Then you notice that the bus is not going its usual way, but is crossing a bridge over a river that you have never seen before. A lion suddenly appears in front of the bus and the bus comes to a halt. You can smell the wild animal outside the bus. You want to shout in panic but you are inaudible to yourself. Then you see that you are the only passenger in the bus and the lion is now in the doorway. You try to run to the second exit, but then your eyes suddenly fly open and the dream ends abruptly.

That is how dreams are—they do not follow a logical sequence. In the aforementioned example, there were people, an animal, a bus, and different locations. Things were happening. There were emotions such as anxiety, fear and frustration. There was a task at hand—to reach the examination hall. There were sensory perceptions like seeing, hearing and smelling. Yet, all that diversity was generated by just one brain—yours. In that tiny space in your head, all those people, emotions and situations existed. Can your brain physically hold all those objects? It is just your brain generating a sequence of images that formed a dream. Material things in the dream were created by a physical brain undergoing sublime biochemical processes and generating subtle things like thought and sensory perception.

Now, notice carefully how you, the dreamer, were one, but the objects in the dream were many. You were the only reality; all those people, the animal and objects in the dream were a falsity. You were real, while those images were unreal. At the same time, that dream and its contents were nothing but a part of you. They were false, but they were you. You, the single entity, projected that multiplicity in your dream. You were anxious, fearful and desperate in your dream, but as soon as you woke up, you realized none of that was real. It was just a temporary projection of your mind. In other words, you and the dream you were witnessing were not two separate things. They were one. Oneness was the truth.

This shift in perspective, this waking up, is the revelation of the truth. In Vedanta, the waking up is the realization of your true nature. When you wake up to the truth, all your pain and suffering automatically comes to an end. You realize that it was the mind–body that was suffering and not you. Vedanta tells you that your true nature is non-dual. It is the one and only reality, and everything is manifested from that reality, including your joys and sorrows. When your mind doubts whether or not you and the universe are the same reality, think of any dream you had and focus on *who* was having that dream.

ARE YOU THE WATER OR THE WAVE?

To further clarify the point, let us take one of the most well-known Vedantic illustrations of non-duality—the imagery of the ocean and the waves. (See Suggested Reading*) Visualize an ocean with an apparently unlimited amount of water in it. Throughout the ocean, the water is the same, but numerous waves rise in that water and fall back into it. Now consider any one wave. That wave, one of many, has its individual existence. It moves, it dances, it is born and it will die. For the time it is there, the wave form is its reality.

Now think deeper. The wave is nothing but the water of

the ocean. It is not separate from the ocean. Further, even the ocean cannot exist without the water. Water is what gives existence to the ocean and its waves. Now, if the wave thought of itself as different from the ocean, would that not be a huge error? The wave cannot exist without the water but the water can exist whether or not there is any wave. The two are non-dual; they are one. The underlying truth of the wave and the ocean is water.

Similarly, Brahman is the reality of all existence, the substance from which everything is projected and into which everything assimilates. If you have any doubt, consider this: Brahman is existence itself. For anything to exist, existence is needed. That is the most fundamental requirement. Thus, the fact that you exist is enough evidence that you are Brahman, just as the wave is the water, the underlying truth of all the waves.

THE STORY OF THE LITTLE WAVE

Here is a simple story, with an extraordinary message,[2] used by teachers of Vedanta. Once, a little wave came into existence in an ocean. As soon as it became aware of itself being a wave, it looked around and started observing. It was happy in its existence till it noticed waves larger than itself. There were waves that were stronger, bigger or higher than itself. Jealously set in and that led to dissatisfaction. When it noticed the bubbles, much smaller, the negative feelings subsided and it felt happy for some time again. This way, its life went on with a mixed bag of feelings and situations, till one day, it saw something that terrorized it.

The wave saw a rocky shore from a distance. It observed

that all the waves that struck the shore disappeared. It got to know of the concept of death and realized that all waves would disappear when they hit the shore. The little wave was depressed at the thought that it too would die one day. It started spending its days in gloom, till one day it met a wise wave. On learning of the little wave's despair, the wise wave said that the waves might appear to be dying at the shore, but their true nature, the reality of their existence, never dies. That immortal reality of the waves is called water. The little wave understood that this entity called water is immortal and numerous waves are projected from it and merge back into it. Waves come and go but water remains. However, it thought, *what about me?* The wise wave said, 'There is no cause for worry, little wave. That immortal reality, the underlying existence called water, is nothing other than you. You are water. You were water and you will be water, even when your wave form dies.'

Similarly, you are Brahman, and you project yourself as this universe and its diverse experiences. Your mind–body form will die, but the ultimate reality, the substratum, will remain. Your reality is never affected by the joys and sorrows that arise in you.

THE POWERFUL ANALOGY OF SPACE

The assertion that everything is consciousness or Brahman and that you are nothing other than this consciousness or Brahman can be further illustrated with the concept of space. Gaudapada explains, 'Though forms, actions, and names differ by respect of the difference in the spaces created by the jars, etc., yet there is no multiplicity in space. So also is the definite conclusion with regard to the individual beings. As the space within a jar is neither a transformation nor a part of space, so an individual being is never a transformation nor a part of the supreme Self.'[3]

The words might seem complicated but the idea is of simple rationality. Consider an earthen pot or a clay jar. When the pot is created, a certain section of the space (that is all around us and we usually perceive it as air) is enclosed in the jar. We refer to it as the space within the jar, while the space external to it is the space outside the jar. But in reality, is there any differentiation between the two spaces at all? Can you divide space? Everything you build is *in* space. If you construct a cardboard box and close its lid, the space inside it is confined by the box. If you dismantle it, will the inner space merge back into the space outside of it? Your instinct will be to say yes, but consider that the differentiation was never there. You had constructed the box in space and when the box did not exist anymore, the space was exactly as it used to be.

Everything that you see is in space. Space, or *akasha* in Sanskrit, is everywhere. Atoms that form all matter are 99.9 per cent space. The entire universe exists in space. Our planet too is in space, though in common understanding, we think space is something that is beyond the horizon of the earth. In addition to what we can see with the naked eye, even with the most powerful telescopes and technology, only five per cent of space is visible to us. That includes all the galaxies and all forms of matter that can exist in outer space. Here on earth, all the plants, animals, objects and humans that exist are in space. Even the human body is 99 per cent empty space, and that body too happens to be *in* space.

Thus, we can see how space is everywhere, inside and outside. All the entities gain existence in it and when they are destroyed, merge back into it. Similarly, Brahman is the only reality of existence. All that we can see, including us, is 'created' from Brahman and 'dissolves' back into Brahman. Yet, like the wave, we are always the ocean. We never were separate from Brahman and will never be outside of it, just like you cannot construct a pot or a box outside of space.

Interestingly, everything that we do not see is also in space. Consider another Vedantic example. On a particular day, small clouds are dotting the sky and you are enjoying the spectacle. One dense cloud moves with the wind and covers the sun. You cannot see the sun now. You think that the cloud is obstructing your view of the sun, when in fact the cloud itself is visible to you only because of the light of the sun. You would not have been able to see the cloud, or anything for that matter, if it were pitch-dark all around you. Similarly, our ignorance of anything is also in Brahman, that is, in our consciousness. It is our consciousness that makes us aware of our lack of awareness. In effect, everything perceivable or not perceivable exists within Brahman.

Brahman is the only reality of the universe. Everything is projected from Brahman and everything goes back to it. These projections take temporary names, forms and usages, but in essence remain Existence-Consciousness-Bliss. Having understood that, what place can there be for any suffering to exist in your mind? The suffering that infiltrates your mind can be taken as a transitory state that cannot and will not touch your inner core, which is true bliss. Yet, we take this suffering to be real and our true nature to be false. The Yoga Vasishtha Sarah exclaims, 'When analyzed, it appears very strange that Brahman, which is of the nature of eternal existence, has been totally forgotten by people, and that ignorance, which is non-existent, is shining before them!'[4]

EXERCISES

The exercises in this chapter go beyond just one activity. These are things that you can work on anywhere, any time. All you need is to focus on the purpose of these exercises. Before you decide to practise these suggestions, remind yourself that you are the witness of everything that you can perceive in your life. When you start practising this frequently, it becomes a habit. And once that habit is formed, you will not be shaken by sorrows or uprooted by happiness. You will find yourself in a calm state most of the time, while responding to situations with the action required.

Here are a few suggestions about the situations in which you can practise this; you can also create your own list to remind yourself of the need to practise this concept. Though these are to be actually practised, you might want to also write your thoughts as you do each exercise.

a) When you feel sad, draw your thoughts to the real 'I' and see yourself from a distance. Tell yourself: 'I, the witness consciousness, am watching this mind having sad thoughts. The thoughts are temporary and will go away. This mind will once again attain its blissful state because I am pure existence, pure consciousness, pure bliss.'

b) When you feel happy, again draw your thoughts to your inner self, the real 'I', and tell yourself, 'I, the witness consciousness, am watching this mind experiencing waves of happiness. This happiness reflects the bliss that I am. The waves will subside, but the ever-present bliss will remain because I am pure existence, pure consciousness, pure bliss.'

c) When you are physically hurt or when you are sick, draw your thoughts to the 'I' inside of you, yet beyond this body, and tell yourself, 'I, the witness consciousness, am watching this body in pain. The pain is temporary. It will subside because I am beyond any suffering. I am pure existence, pure consciousness, pure bliss.'

14

THE ENIGMA CALLED MAYA

Now comes the most intriguing part of our quest for the ultimate truth. Some fundamental questions might have been following you throughout the previous chapter. Why, at all, does Brahman appear in all this diversity? If the reality is one, why does it appear as many? If there is one consciousness pervading the entire universe, then why does such a tremendous amount of diversity appear? If our true nature is bliss, then why does this mind–body experience pain and suffering? Why at all are we ignorant of our true nature and have to take the trouble of journeying back to understanding our true nature?

These questions are logical and valid. Interestingly, these questions will remain with us even when we have been provided with numerous explanations, except under one condition. And that is seeing for ourselves. The reason is this: we, with the way our minds are conditioned, cannot accept that anything that is originally blissful should take on forms that are highly unpleasant. With the human instinct for survival, we want to preserve the pleasant and banish the unpleasant. Why then would we, Brahman, have wanted to create death, disease and old age? If we are Brahman, why would we have wanted ourselves to suffer?

The conundrum is that any answer that we are given sounds unsatisfactory because of this very conditioning of our minds. The same answers will lead to lasting peace if the mind is conditioned to receive this knowledge. It can be either way, depending on which way your mind is leaning. It is noteworthy here that though the Absolute is beyond the mind, the mind is a necessary tool to reach that reality. It is only through our intellect that the preliminary comprehension will awaken, and only after that will we be able to perceive the reality. This is also why the mind is called the *antahkarna* or 'inner instrument' in Vedanta. At the same time, one of the faculties of the mind, the ego, blocks our understanding of the true nature of reality. This is a multi-layered problem and to solve it, let us propose a simple solution—let us keep our ego-identity in the back seat and let our intellect take charge. Holding on to this arrangement, let us explore how this mystery has been explained through the centuries by the greatest Vedantic scholars.

THE QUESTION OF GOD

Before we explore questions on the origin of the universe, let us look at the common notions that we have. To address the mystery of creation, or why this world exists at all, religion presents a simplistic answer—it is God who creates the world and only God knows all the mysteries of the world. If we are followers of a religion, we tend to place our belief in an all-powerful entity that directs the workings of this world. In Vedanta, however, the description of God is subtler. God in Vedanta is defined in ways distinct from religion.

Vedanta is primarily a spiritual philosophy, and there are subtle differences between religion and spirituality. As I stated in my book *Vediquant* (2023), 'If spirituality is like water, religion is like ice.'[1] Just like free-flowing water, spirituality is not bound by shapes and laws. Religion, on the other hand, like ice, needs particular conditions to maintain its form. Both, however, intersect at numerous points, leading to a blurring of lines between them. Vedanta too faces the same situation. Therefore, you might assume that there would be a conflict between the concept of God and the concept of Brahman.

However, there is no conflict. In fact, there are delicate differentiations. The formless, all-pervading, absolute truth, without attributes or qualities, is named Brahman; it is the substance from which everything appears to be created. When Brahman appears with attributes like space, time and causation, it assumes the form of God and is referred to as Ishvara, Hiranyagarbha, and like terms. So, the attribute-less Absolute appears in the perceivable universe as God, with form and function. The formless absolute is called Nirguna Brahman and the aspect with attributes is called Saguna Brahman. The latter is a personal God and can be addressed with various names.

Therefore, the definitions of God in Vedanta differ from those given in religion. These are often encapsulated in the mahavakyas. One such definition mentions the Absolute as *Satyam Gyanam Anantam Brahman*.[2] Brahman is truth, knowledge and infinite, and that is God. Another definition is even subtler: *Pragyanam Brahman*[3]—Consciousness is Brahman. As we have seen, everything is consciousness and is within consciousness, therefore the Ultimate Reality is consciousness, call it Brahman or God. A consolidation of non-duality is found in this definition: *tat tvam asi*—That Thou Art.[4] The real you is nothing other than the Absolute. You are That. The same assertion is mentioned as *ayam atma brahma*—This Self is Brahman.[5]

Thus, by whichever name we call it, there is one absolute reality and it is the one that projects all this diversity of name, form and action into this universe. Does Brahman do this itself? Does Brahman act or work to make things happen? The answer is no. This immutable entity does not indulge in action. Then how does it create all this? Here enters a mysterious concept that has befuddled scholars for ages. The parameters are unthinkable—the changeless Brahman is projected as this breathtaking diversity we see in the universe. How is this even possible?

MAYA—THE QUINTESSENTIAL ENIGMA

The explanation for the above conundrum is maya. It is a grandiose, mystical power of Brahman that projects the formless as something with form. Maya is an incredibly difficult concept to grasp. It is not real but it is not unreal either. It is said to be existing, yet non-existent. In other words, it is a positive nothing. Maya is used synonymously with avidya, ignorance of the truth.

The complexity is that maya is present in the unreal but is absent in the real. To get a peek into this, let us get back to the example of the snake and the rope. When you mistake the rope for a snake, it is the work of avidya or maya. The latter makes you believe that there is a snake in front of you.

A person who encounters a mirage in a desert and believes it is water is under the spell of maya. The latter makes one believe that an illusion is the truth. Since ignorance itself is nothing, maya can be said to be non-existent. Yet, it works in strange ways to present this world before us.

Maya has two roles: that of creation and that of veiling. The word 'creation' is not to be taken literally. In absolute terms, there is no creation at all. The world is only an illusory appearance of the truth, which is Brahman, just like the water in the mirage, which is not there in reality. Yet, while this illusion lasts, it is real. That is why it is a transitory truth, and hence, only one aspect of the absolute truth. This illusion of reality is the work of maya. This is its creative power with which it makes the world appear along with its unlimited names and forms. Due to this, maya is also sometimes referred to as *Prakriti* or Nature. It generates a world before us, complete with living and non-living objects, with bodies and minds, and with physical phenomena unfolding before us. We are bound in an endless cycle of desire and action because of the world presented to us. This 'creation' is the apparent truth for us, and we spend our lives believing that this is all. As Gaudapada mentions in the *Mandukya Karika*, 'The self-effulgent Self imagines Itself through Itself by the power of Its own Maya. The Self Itself cognizes the objects. Such is the definitive conclusion of Vedanta.'[6]

In addition to 'creating' a world before us, Maya is particularly effective in veiling the truth from us. That is its second function. It keeps the truth under wraps. As a result, we are unable to see our real nature. This illusory world is called *samsara* in Sanskrit. A person trapped in samsara (and all of us are) believes this world to be the reality. Till the time you believe the rope to be a snake, maya is hiding the truth from you. The moment you awaken to the fact that it is a rope, the spell of maya is broken and you are free of samsara. Freedom from samsara means the end of all suffering. When you realize the truth about the snake, you are no longer fearful. When you wake up from a nightmare, you realize that what you mistook for reality was in fact just a false projection. The result is freedom from despair.

It is important to note a subtle fact here. While the illusion lasts, you will and you should act according to the requirement of the situation. In a dream, if there is a fire in the house, you (in the dream) must make an attempt to put it out. If you are experiencing this world created by maya, you must act according to the best of your ability. Since you have the name and form of a human being, you must do all the right things human beings are supposed to do.

Here is another subtle point—when you know your true nature, working through samsara becomes easier. You are able to face sadness and happiness without getting flustered by either. That is the awakening, the highest purpose of human life. You might encounter the same rope again and, for a moment, take it to be a snake, but now that you know better, you will not be fearful of that transitory illusion. This way, you have understood the role of maya. The Yoga Vasishtha Sarah presents this idea succinctly, 'This creation, which is merely the form of a vibration of Consciousness alone, is dissolved by accurate knowledge and again arises with false knowledge, just as the false knowledge of the snake arises upon the rope.'[7]

If you have noticed, the emphasis is upon right

knowledge. What is right knowledge? Can knowledge be false? Again, when we are talking in terms of absolute reality, whatever is transitory is false and whatever is permanent is true. The illusion of the water in the mirage was the knowledge you had in that moment, but it turned out to be false when you realized it was just a play of light. In effect, all your troubles and also your joys are 'created' by Maya, and hence are illusions.

BUT WHAT IS MAYA ITSELF?

What exactly is Maya itself? Nothing is outside of Brahman; hence maya is an aspect of the Absolute. It is not an independent entity. It is a power of Brahman that projects the changeless Brahman into this entire universe along with its myriad manifestations, names and forms. Does this mean that maya 'transforms' or 'moulds' Brahman into these objects? Absolutely not. The immutable is beyond maya, so it remains untouched by its actions, just like you may have all kinds of dreams, but you remain as you are. An accident in the dream does not hurt the real you, and the money you get in the dream does not make you any richer. Brahman remains unscathed by the functioning of maya. An entity that is beyond the powerful maya, beyond all vibrations of sadness and even happiness, and all mutations of consciousness imaginable, is bound to invoke reverence and awe.

The clay pot example comes in handy once again to explain maya. Consider a pot made of clay. The clay has been shaped into a form, that of the pot. The pot has a function, which in ancient times was to store water or grain. The form and function give the pot an identity, in which it 'lives' its life. However, the fundamental truth of the pot is clay. The same clay must have been formed into another utensil, or a brick, or a plate. These objects have their individual identities till the time they have their respective forms. What happens when the pot breaks? It turns into clay again. The clay remains, the pot is gone. If all those objects are destroyed, the clay will still remain. The individual names and forms will die; their absolute reality will remain.*

Now, consider the gold jewellery example again. The necklace, bangle and ring made of gold would have different forms and functions, which are their identities for the moment. If they were sentient, they could have had egos and, hence, would have struggled to establish who was superior, bigger or more powerful. When the pieces are melted in a workshop, what remains is only the gold. The individual forms and functions are gone; only their underlying reality remains.

Likewise, the underlying reality of existence is one—Brahman. This absolute reality is projected as the multitude of objects and creatures in this universe. That is the work

---

*The clay pot is one of the most effective examples in Vedanta, but often objections are raised against it based on an incomplete understanding or a misunderstanding of the example. One objection is that it is not just the clay, but the water and other binding materials too that form the pot. The other one is that the clay is heat-dried and cannot merge back into the original clay. It is best to ignore these points because no analogy is perfect. We can find dozens of inconsistencies in every analogy, which would be a fruitless activity because the purpose of every analogy is to illustrate a certain point. It is best to take the example in the singular context in which it is being mentioned.

of maya. The fundamental reality is revealed when the veil of maya is lifted. And the only way to do it is through knowledge. The only thing that can remove your illusion of the snake is to see the rope for yourself. There may be other people trying to convince you that it is just a rope, but nothing will work till you recognize the rope yourself. That is why Vedanta insists on direct realization instead of just relying on what you hear or learn, hence *nididhyasana*. It is up to you to lift the veil and see the hidden reality. Maya will try its best not to let that happen, but in the presence of knowledge, it vanishes in a moment. Says Sage Vasishtha to his disciple Prince Rama, 'O Rama, this Maya (the cause of this creation) is such that it gives joy to itself through its own destruction. Its nature (what it actually is) is neither observable nor understandable; if one sees (with a discriminating eye), then it cannot be found at all. It is destroyed. (That is why Maya is indeterminable).'[8]

MAYA'S ARSENAL—TIME, SPACE, CAUSATION AND GUNAS

Vedanta tells us that our reality is Brahman, unchanging, unmoving and unaffected by joys and sorrows, but maya hides it and shows us only the transitory reality, which includes our feelings and emotions, and the pain and suffering that the body is experiencing. How does maya achieve this? Why do we get a sense of things changing with time? Why is every person different from every other person? Why, in spite of being told about our true nature, can we not see it?

Maya is inscrutable, but its workings can be perceived

through the aspects of *desha*, *kala* and *nimitta*—space, time and causation, respectively. Brahman, and in effect the real you, are limitless. Maya creates the illusion of this limited mind and body placed in a physical universe. You, the Atman, are timeless, but maya makes you believe that there is something called the flow of time. The time period between two events is considered as the indication that time is real, and that time flows from past to the future. In Vedanta, space and time are not real. These are illusions created by maya.

The same concept is echoed in the modern findings of quantum physics, where space and time are not absolutes. The bending of space-time gives positions to objects, and no object has any specific position in the cosmos, be it galaxies or our own little Earth. Time is relative, and would tick differently for a person on Earth and another one on a spaceship. The 'observer problem' in quantum mechanics, where the observer and observed are connected to each other, also finds echoes in Vedanta, where it is Brahman only that appears as the entire universe (See Suggested Reading*). There is no duality. Just like the space in the pot was never separate from the space outside of it, Brahman never acquired any form or shape. It was always unchanged.

The same is true for the concept of causation. Since there is only one reality that is the substratum of everything, there is no scope for one thing to come after another. In other words, cause and effect are illusions created by maya. This is a mind-bending concept for sure. Another Vedantic example comes to our rescue in understanding it. Think of a seed that grows into a sprout and then into a plant which becomes a tree. Was the seed a 'cause' of the tree? The tree was always there in the seed, wasn't it? It had just not taken the *form* of a tree. You were once a baby. Is your infancy the 'cause', and the present body the 'effect' of that cause? That is illogical because the baby was exactly what you are right now. This baffling appearance and the resulting confusion are the workings of maya. Thus, Gaudapada draws attention to this crucial aspect: 'After realizing cause-lessness as the truth, and not accepting any separate cause, one attains the state of fearlessness that is free from sorrow and devoid of desire.'[9]

Maya also gives different entities their unique characteristics. In its creative role, maya works through three qualities—*sattva*, *rajas* and *tamas*—called *guna*s. These are like fundamental operating principles that maya solicits to give a particular nature to an entity. These qualities are associated primarily with sentient creatures, and in the highest degree with humans. Sattva denotes knowledge, purity and calmness; rajas represents ambition, restlessness and passion; and tamas leads to ignorance, laziness and negative qualities like hatred, jealousy and arrogance. The three gunas are present in varying proportions in each individual. It is up to the individual to alter the proportions to attain a certain kind of a personality. Once a person becomes aware of these, they can attain the right balance of these qualities. It is important to note that the only way to do that is through knowledge.

WHY MAYA?

Living in a world created by maya, it is difficult to comprehend maya. Yet, Vedantic scholars have provided explanations that might throw some light on the nature of maya, depending on where we stand in our perception of reality. Just like the very nature of Brahman is existence, the very nature of maya is to create and to hide. This is why it indulges in this play of time, space and causation, coloured by the three gunas. Another perspective is that unless maya projects a false world before us, we will not be able to see the truth. Through our minds, we comprehend the false, and hence get a vision of the real. Thus, maya helps us comprehend the truth.

Yet another insight is provided by Sri Ramakrishna Paramahamsa, who said that maya can be of two types—vidya maya and avidya maya. The latter is the one that keeps us away from reality, but the former is the path to reaching the truth. It is through gaining vidya, or knowledge of our true identity, that we are set free from falsity. Knowledge itself is the domain of maya, but in this case, it helps. Thus, the way to transcend maya is *through* maya.[10]

THE PRINCESS OF KASHI

A famous Vedantic parable beautifully illustrates the role of maya. The story is set in ancient India. Once, a king's court organized the presentation of a theatrical play. One of the characters in that play was the little princess of Kashi. The organizers could not find a little girl to play that role, so the king's son, a child at that time, was dressed up as a princess. When the queen saw her son looking extremely pretty in the guise of a little girl, she asked the royal painter to paint a portrait of the child. The painter created a lovely picture, put the date on it and labelled the painting 'Princess of Kashi'. As years passed by, the painting was forgotten and stored away with other items in the palace basement.

Meanwhile, the child grew up into a young man, training for his duties as a prince. As it happens with everyone, he had very few memories of his early childhood. Consequently, he had forgotten that incident too. One day, while he was in the palace basement, the prince chanced upon the painting. He was captivated by the beauty of the princess of Kashi. He saw the date documented on the painting, calculated, and figured out that the girl in the painting must be almost his age now. So enamoured was he with the face in the painting, that he could not help thinking about her day and night.

People around him noticed that the prince seemed to be strangely preoccupied. The king and the queen were worried. The prince, out of shyness, would not share his infatuation with his parents. The king then asked his wisest minister, now an elderly official, to talk to the prince and find out the reason behind his strange quietness. When the minister encouraged the prince to share his thoughts, the prince said, 'I think I am in love.' The minister was not just relieved, but happy on learning that the girl was a princess, something that would make the match easier. When the eager minister asked for further details, it turned out that the prince had only seen a painting and was madly in love.

When the prince took the minister to the painting, the latter recognized it, and recalled the event that had led to it. Baffled at first, the minister slowly revealed the facts to the prince. Finally, he said, 'Therefore, dear prince, the princess of Kashi is none other than you!' The prince was at first shocked, but when he realized that the object of his desire was nothing other than himself, his desire vanished. As a result, his despair and suffering also went away.[11]

According to the 'Vaitathya Prakarna' of the *Mandukya Karika*, 'There is no dissolution, no origination, none in bondage, none striving or aspiring for salvation and none liberated. This is the highest truth.'[12] You, the witness consciousness, project yourself as this Universe through Maya, and get trapped in the cycle of desires, joys and sorrows. When you realize you are in reality never affected by anything, you find the solution to your suffering.

EXERCISE

For this exercise, we are going to take verses from the Ashtavakra Samhita, a profound and poetic description of the state of reality and the predicament we all experience. Sage Ashtavakra indicates to his disciple, King Janaka, the method to realize oneself as the witness consciousness.

The particular verse mentioned below is infused with peace and bliss. Just visualizing its imagery would bring your mind to a state of calm. Now is the right time to practise this, because by this stage in the book, you are familiar with the terms and the concepts being mentioned here.

> In me, the limitless ocean, let the wave of the world rise or vanish of itself. I neither increase nor decrease thereby.[13]

Read the above verse part by part, visualize it and try to imbibe the import. Here are a few suggestions to help you. Imagine yourself as the water of the ocean, boundless, free and immensely powerful. It may help you to mentally place yourself in the water and see yourself as the ocean.

Imagine a wave of sadness rising in your water. It goes up, stays for some time and falls back. See where it falls. It falls back right into *you*. Imagine something that made you joyous. See that joy rising from your water like a wave, dancing around, and then falling back. Where did that joy fall back? Right into you again. Similarly, recall the different painful experiences you have had. Imagine them as waves in you, the ocean. Those experiences will rise and fall. *You* will remain. If you want to, write down your thoughts about this experience.

_____
_____
_____
_____
_____
_____
_____
_____
_____
_____
_____
_____
_____

When you have visualized the above, come to the following verse, also from the Ashtavakra Samhita, and read it out to yourself, absorbing the meaning slowly:

> In me, the boundless ocean, is the imagination of the universe. I am quite tranquil and formless. In this alone do I abide.[13]

Now close your eyes and tell yourself that you, the tranquil, calm, peaceful ocean will not be disturbed by the waves rising in you. The waves are on the surface. The depths of you are forever tranquil. Let the sadness, the misery, the grief, the pain and the emotions rise like waves on your surface. Deep within, you remain calm.

It is not necessary, but if you want, you can write down how you felt during this visualization.

_____
_____
_____
_____
_____
_____
_____
_____
_____
_____
_____
_____
_____
_____
_____

15

THE REALIZATION—THE END OF ALL SUFFERING

At this point in your journey to the summit, the view has changed dramatically. You have taken giant steps that have brought you from a recognition of your suffering to knowing what suffering is in relation to your reality. At this step, you can see that all the previous steps were but sub-parts of this stage that you are at right now. You can see all the previous levels merging into this one. Yet, unless you had taken the first step, you would not have been here.

The view from here is surreal, but ironically, that which sounds unreal is the real *you*. Maya has blocked your access to the unlimited bliss within you. At the same time, this maya will vanish in a moment if you shine the light of your understanding on it. If you can look beyond maya, the latter itself will help you see the reality that you truly are. Says the Isha Upanishad, 'When to the person of realization all beings become the very Self then what delusion and what sorrow can there be for that seer of oneness?'[1]

TAT TVAM ASI—THAT THOU ART

That is the nature of your reality in Advaita Vedanta. The highest Truth is nothing other than you. You are Brahman, consciousness, Atman. That thou art—That you are. You are the one that illumines all the experiences. While the word 'illumine' sounds poetic and vague, it basically means that it is because of your consciousness that you experience everything in the universe. To illumine means to reveal, or to make perceivable, not to shine like material light.

A logical question arises here. What about the countless objects, people and mental processes in the universe that you are not aware of? You do not know all of them, so how can they be in your consciousness? Here is a stunning claim: everything that you know and also everything that you do not know is in your consciousness. Differentiating between knowledge and awareness can help us understand this crucial point. Knowledge is in your mind. It comprises the things that you empirically know through observation, study or casual reference. On the other hand, awareness is pure existence. Existence is everywhere, whether or not you have the knowledge of all its contents. Therefore, all that is known and all that is unknown exists in you as awareness.

When this realization dawns, there is no cause left for sadness. When you are the universe, what more is there for you to desire or acquire? All sadness and happiness rise within you and fall into you as temporary waves. Just like the space within a jar is not affected by whatever is poured into the jar—poison or nectar—you are never in reality affected by any pain or suffering. You remain as Existence, Consciousness, Bliss, even when misery and grief strike you.

In truth, it is the one immutable existence that is the underlying truth. Suffering will last as long as illusion lasts. Swami Vivekananda had called for the 'dehypnotization' of our minds. Under the hypnotic spell of maya, we are not able to see beyond the physical pain and the suffering mind. We think this is all. In reality, you are untouched by any pain or suffering.

THE NUANCES—THE PRACTICAL ASPECTS

At this point, you might still think that since you feel the pinch on your arm or the hot sun on your skin, the world cannot possibly be false. That is perfectly fine. Vedanta does not want to erase the experience of the world from your mind. It wants you to understand the experience. It does not matter if you believe the rope to be a snake for some time. It will, however, matter if you saw the reality of the rope yet chose to live in fear of the false snake.

There is a reason why our experience of the world exists, why we are able to recognize pain and pleasure. If our body and mind had no role, we would have done very well to have existed simply as an abstract formless existence. That would have been quite a monotonous state. Though we do not know *why* Brahman appears as all these forms, we do know that it *does* appear in all this variety. And we can be glad about it, for it is because of this that we experience numerous shades of living, the myriad colours and flavours of existence.

Consider these experiences of life like play-dough, or like modelling clay that children use to make different forms and shapes. A child moulds the same clay into a ball, a wand, a car, an animal, and believes it to be that respective object for some time. The objects too play their part. When they are flattened and merged back into the clay that they came from, they lose their temporary identity. Yet, they were always clay and will always be clay. If any of those objects clung to its form, it would limit its existence. Take the toy car, for instance, modelled out of that dough. To play its role, it would need to maintain its shape, it would need someone to move it, and it would need washing to look fresh. But is that all? Is that the truth behind its existence? What if the car insisted that its form is real and there is nothing beyond it called clay or dough?

The solution is to not deny that there is something beyond the experiences that we have. We will not be able to describe it, but we can be aware of it. Our physical and mental experiences will continue, but we will know that the suffering that comes with these experiences is not the actual truth, only a transitory one.

Contemporary consciousness studies are slowly unravelling what Vedanta is pointing towards (though the two disciplines are widely different and it would be an error to assume that one is being influenced by the other). Science is moving towards an understanding of the nature of consciousness, or at least its components. The term used for the units of consciousness is 'qualia'. Qualia are supposed to be ineffable, which means it is difficult to define or describe them. They can be known only by direct experience, just like the Upanishads mention. Qualia do not change in contact or in relation with any other entity, which is the very definition of Brahman. It is like saying that one can perceive it but one cannot define it. (See Suggested Reading*)

These descriptions of the basic units of consciousness find echoes in the Kena Upanishad:

> That which is not uttered by speech, that by which speech is revealed, know that alone to be Brahman... That which a person does not see with the eye, that by which the person perceives the activities of the eye, know that alone to be Brahman... That which a person does not comprehend with the mind, that by which, they say, the mind is encompassed, know that to be Brahman... That which a person does not smell with the organ of smell, that by which the organ of smell is impelled, know that to be Brahman...[1]

Simply put, you are the reality behind all that you perceive. The experiences will change; you will remain constant. The sadness, depression, anxiety or pain that you feel are just bubbles on the surface of you, the ocean. These are transitory, and you are aware of them because you are awareness itself.

YOUR SUPERPOWERS

Since you are existence itself, the immutable consciousness, and your very nature is bliss, your real nature is blessed with immense superpowers. A word of caution here. These superpowers are not like the temporal powers that humans think they wield in the world. To even recognize these powers, you have to undertake a journey like you have been taking in this workbook. When you identify these powers, you will need to practise to attune your mind into their working. When you can fully appreciate these powers, you will achieve the most desirable thing in life—you will transcend suffering.

The best manifestation of your superpowers is viveka, a Sanskrit word that means discernment, the ability to differentiate between the real and the unreal, which is immensely powerful. You will still feel pain and hurt, but you will not be rattled by such things. In spite of the severest of pain, disease or suffering, you will remain calm and blissful. Like Dattatreya in the *Avadhuta Gita*, you can sing, 'Truly I am Brahman, free from passion, jealousy, hatred and the rest. I am that reality devoid of sufferings caused by physical, terrestrial, and supernatural agencies. I am that Truth untouched by grief and misery of the world. I am Existence-Knowledge-Bliss and boundless as space.'[2]

The most intense aspect of your superpowers is the absence of fear. Imagine the most powerful person in the world. Even if they had all the power in every way possible, they could still be fearful. The most powerful person is one who does not have fear. This is what Vedanta promises you. When you know what is real and what is unreal, the latter cannot disturb your peace of mind. You will be able to transcend fear every time it arises. According to the Taittiriya Upanishad, 'One is not subjected to fear at any time if one knows the Bliss that is Brahman.'[3]

Even the greatest of all fears, the fear of death, subsides when you make your mind stable in the knowledge of Brahman. The Katha Upanishad paints a vivid picture of this assertion: 'One becomes freed from the jaws of death by knowing that which is soundless, touchless, colourless, undiminishing, and also tasteless, eternal, odourless, without beginning, and without end, distinct from Mahat, and ever constant.'[4] The word *mahat* here denotes intelligence or buddhi, thus indicating that this entity is not perceivable even by the intellect. This signifies that your true self does not change with changing perceptions. It remains steady in its state of pure bliss.

You could still be facing the troubles that life throws at you, but this transcendental nature of your true self cannot be harmed by anything. 'Just as the sun, which is the eye of the whole world, is not tainted by the ocular and external defects, similarly, the Self, that is but one in all beings, is not tainted by the sorrows of the world, It being transcendental.'[5] The light of the sun aids the vision of everything in the world, hence the expression the 'eye of the world'.

The analogy is striking. The light of the sun touches everything in the world, including excreta, dirt and toxic substances. Yet, it does not get tainted by that contact. The light does not become impure by touching a dirty object. It remains as it is. It shines upon all objects and makes their presence perceivable. Yet, it is not affected by any quality of those objects. Similarly you, the witness consciousness, are illumining all experiences, including those of misery, suffering and distress, yet you are never really affected by them. Thus, your true nature is self-effulgent—it shines in its own light and is not dependent on anything else.

This is succinctly summed up in the Yoga Vasishtha Sarah: 'Just as the wind is incapable of shaking a painting of a creeper, similarly, the intellect (purified with extreme tenacity) that is fastened in the mirror of discrimination and has thus attained steadiness, cannot be shaken by disease, mental sufferings, and the like.'[6]

EXERCISES

Since we have expressed the highest truth in this chapter, the exercises would be of a nature that you can practise throughout your day, while in the middle of a routine. Read these suggestions and try to implement them whenever a similar situation arises in your life. You can write down your thoughts in this space later. These are indicative exercises to get you started. You may further design similar ones for yourself.

a) When you are experiencing illness or disease, tell yourself that it is the body that is sick. It will feel the pain and the discomfort, but that will pass. In spite of the physical suffering, you have the power to maintain peace in your mind. Tell yourself that you will do all that is necessary—seek medical advice, take medication—but smile at the thought that this is temporary.

_____
_____
_____
_____
_____

b) When you are distressed because of failure or emotional hurt, tell yourself that it is the mind that is experiencing these emotions. You, the witness, are watching your mind going through these sad thoughts, and this too shall pass.

_____
_____
_____

c) When you feel your mind getting unsettled due to desires of more money, possessions, praise or credit, tell yourself that your true self is way beyond these temporary things. Tell yourself that you will continue to make efforts to achieve more, but deep inside, you will not feel unsettled if that does not happen. You, the vast ocean, will not be reduced by the lack of a few waves.

16

A DANGER AND A WARNING

At this stage, your mind will be grappling with an inevitable question. If you are the universe, and if you are self-sufficient, never changing, if you are the Absolute, then why do you need to perform any action? If the entire world is an appearance created by maya, if none of this is real, then you may as well sit back and let it pass. Why should you bother about success, health and happiness? Your real nature is complete in all senses, then why the hard work and the striving to achieve goals? Why make the effort to keep the body healthy, earn money for a better life, or excel at your profession?

If you are puzzled by similar ideas, you are not alone. Through the ages, even the greatest minds have faced similar predicaments. This is where Vedanta provides you with practical solutions, and the perfect balance between knowledge of the Absolute and the management of worldly life. To gain knowledge of the ultimate reality is not to negate the experience of this world. Countless times in Vedantic literature, scholars have emphasized the need to respect and value this empirical experience while keeping in mind the absolute reality.

THE NEED FOR ACTION

There are numerous examples and ancient stories that illustrate how this apparent paradox can be resolved. King Janaka was a disciple of the great sage Ashtavakra. Janaka was the knower of the truth, an enlightened being, yet he performed his duties with utmost efficiency. His duties were of the most worldly nature imaginable—that of ruling a kingdom. That meant managing everything from money to politics, to war. His method was to look at all his experiences from the Vedantic perspective of oneness, non-duality. Hence, he was given the title of Sage-King. Janaka says, 'I have extracted from the inmost recesses of my heart the thorn of different opinion, using the pincers of the knowledge of Truth.'[1] This follows an interesting practical instruction by his teacher, Ashtavakra: 'The wise one who lives on happily doing what comes to him to be done, does not feel eagerness either in activity or in inactivity.'[2]

In a different setting, Sage Vasishtha gives advice to Prince Rama in the same vein. Legend has it that Prince Rama wanted to renounce the world and live only in the truth. His father, King Dasharatha, was worried, so he requested Sage Vasishtha to counsel the young Rama. Thus started a dialogue between the two, which was consolidated by an unknown ancient author into a voluminous text called the Yoga Vasishtha Sarah. Such is the depth of insight that has been explained with practical observations and stories that the book is considered a text for enlightenment.

While imparting this highest teaching, Vasishtha helps Rama see that the best choice is to stay in your role in life, and to perform your duties without getting attached to them.

In other words, to do everything that is a part of life while, at the same time, remaining stabilized in the knowledge of the truth. Says Vasishtha:

> Dear Raghava, you roam around the world being free from effort inwardly while apparently energetic outside, keeping the strong conviction of non-doership within while behaving outwardly as a doer... Dear Raghava, you roam around in this world performing all types of actions outwardly, being free from all types of hankering bereft of longing for all worldly objects, and devoid of all desires inwardly.[3]

These words might seem complex in meaning, but the import is simple. It is about being anchored in your true self while outwardly behaving as if you are totally involved with the world. There are nuances here. While performing the actions of the world, you are respecting whatever roles come your way, whether in your personal life or in your profession. You give everything your best, energetically, as Vasishtha says, but deep inside, you always remain calm because you know that those practical things that you are doing are neither adding to you nor taking anything away from you. You do not need anything and you do not fear anything.

KARMA YOGA

The best-known example of this instruction, however, is that of the dialogue between Arjuna and Krishna. In the spectacular setting of a war about to begin between two great armies, the key warrior Arjuna feels incapacitated with doubts and apprehensions. His predicament is not a minor one. He has to battle with members of his extended family, people he loves and respects. Krishna, being a manifestation of the Absolute, acquaints Arjuna with the knowledge of the truth, explaining the differences between the real and the unreal, the immutable and the transitory. When Arjuna gains insight into the ultimate reality, he speaks for all us by expressing this doubt: if knowledge of the Absolute is the only thing worth striving for, then why should he engage in worldly actions like fighting the war and thus causing grief and sadness to himself and to others? He expresses this conundrum: would it not be better to renounce the world and live a life of peace and quietude?

What follows is the loftiest expression of practical advice given to not just Arjuna but all of humanity, making the Bhagavad Gita the seminal text for understanding karma yoga over the centuries. A proper understanding of this hands-on approach to balancing spirituality and practicality is the key to lasting happiness and bliss. Like Arjuna, we all might harbour this doubt—if knowledge of our true nature is superior to all worldly action, then why should we continue with our jobs, our duties and the roles we find ourselves in?

An important thing to note here is that in our human environment, action has gained a bad reputation. Any action will have consequences, and the latter will vary according to the nature of the action taken. This leads to confusion as to what differentiates good actions from bad actions. In a subjective context, this leads to chaos. Thus, when a person gains knowledge of their true, underlying reality, their instinctive reaction is to try to live in that state of bliss, and renounce this world where action needs to be performed.

This, says Krishna, is the most undesirable of things to do. Such avoidance of worldly action is not true renunciation. It is simply an escape and will not do you any good. Then he explains something crucial—the path to true renunciation is *through* action. 'A person does not attain freedom from action by abstaining from action; nor does he attain fulfilment merely through renunciation.'[4]

Then what is the way? How can we ensure that our actions do not result in bondage to sorrow and suffering? This is the solution: 'But, O Arjuna, one who engages in karma yoga with the organs of action, controlling the organs with the mind and becoming unattached—that one excels.'[5] If you are in control of your desires, through the control of your senses, you can attain detachment even while in the middle of action.

Now, how is that possible? Here is a fine point. If you perform the action for the action's sake, and not with the desire of getting a particular result, then you will not be caught in the vicious cycle. This apparently simple suggestion is quite hard to put into practice, but the promised result is glorious. This is the path to finding bliss, the path to freedom from suffering.

And why is that? Why is detached action the path to freedom and bliss? As we have seen while journeying through this book, your true nature is immutable. You are the never-changing Brahman. That true Self is never involved in action. It does not suffer or experience transitory joy. It remains in the state of permanent, unchanging bliss. The world is projected from that unchanging Self by maya and is perceived by our senses.

Thus, to think that in reality you are doing or not doing

something is an error. If you avoid this error, you remain happy. This is echoed in the famous paradoxical verse from the Bhagavad Gita, 'He who finds inaction in action, and action in inaction, he is the wise one.'[6]

This complex statement is simplified by Adi Shankaracharya, who gives the fine example of how when a boat is sailing on the river, the stationary trees on the bank seem to move in the opposite direction. He uses another example to further simplify this: that of a moving object very far from us that seems to be almost motionless.

These two examples illustrate how the wise person knows that even when they appear to be involved in activities, they are actually not doing anything. Moreover, not doing anything is also action. Thus, says Shankaracharya, 'In reality, actions done by a person of knowledge are certainly inactions, since he is endowed with the realization of the actionless Self.'[7] That is the best way to carry on with your life—take on whatever action comes your way, while keeping the truth always in sight. Ashtavakra encapsulates this magic formula in a few words when he says that the wise live in the Self and play the game of life.[8] Ashtavakra's statement draws a roadmap for all of us: to give our best to whatever roles we find ourselves in, and, at the same time, stay centred in the knowledge that our true nature is forever unaffected; it is bliss itself.

EXERCISE

This exercise aims to help us acquire a better understanding of action and inaction, which will underscore the necessity of devoting our lives to unattached karma.

a) Make a list of at least ten things that you do in a day. These could be anything from ordinary things like doing your laundry to more substantive things that are a part of your life.

_____
_____
_____
_____
_____
_____
_____
_____
_____
_____

b) Sort out the activities according to routine work and important work. The latter would fall into the category of karma.

_____
_____
_____
_____
_____
_____
_____
_____
_____

c) When you write or say 'I do this...', notice who is doing that task. It would be your body, mind or senses. Draw your attention to yourself, who is the witness of these actions. Notice how that one never does anything; it only observes.

d) Write down a few things that you decided not to do, like not eating because you were fasting, or not going for a walk because you were resting.

e) Think about and write down how the 'not doing' was also some kind of action.

_____
_____
_____
_____
_____
_____
_____
_____
_____

f) Pay attention to the real you, the witness, observing your body and mind 'not doing' that thing.

_____
_____

g) When you pay attention to the observer, the real you, hold on to that understanding. Internalize it so that you can recall it whenever you find your mind unsettled by something. You may write your thoughts about this entire exercise, or you can simply practise the visualization.

_____
_____
_____
_____
_____
_____

17

THE 'HOW' QUESTION

When Krishna or Vasishtha or Ashtavakra advise their respective disciples on the need for unattached action, the question that immediately arises is *how*? How can one be detached when one is actually experiencing pain in the body or suffering in the mind? Even when one knows that the real Self is unaffected by any despair or misery, even when one understands the need to focus on the eternal reality instead of the temporary suffering, the perplexity stems from how to practise it. Although there are multiple suggestions in Vedantic literature that go in depth into the working of this concept, two in particular stand out because these are more directly applicable to people like us, who are busy with regular lives. One of these is the path of religious devotion.

DEVOTION OR BHAKTI

After explaining the finer aspects of the ultimate knowledge to Arjuna, towards the end of this discourse in the Bhagavad Gita, Krishna sums up a comparatively easier-to-follow method of practising karma yoga. However, this method is only for those who are of a religious bent of mind or at least have a theistic inclination. He suggests that whatever action one may undertake in life, if one submits that work as an offering to God, one will not get entangled in the quagmire of actions and their results.

How does this work? Primarily, this is the subjugation of the ego-identity to your true Self. All the work that you apparently do is done by your body and mind, which are in turn controlled by Nature, and the latter is in effect only a projection of Brahman. Thus, in reality, there is nothing that your ego-identity is doing, though it seems to be functioning that way. As we have seen, maya creates this world of thoughts, emotions, physical actions and everything that is perceived. You, the true Self, Atman, which a devotee may call God, are the reality that is projecting all this. In maya, you think and act, and maya is but a power of Brahman.

Therefore, by offering all your work and thoughts to God, you are paying obeisance to the Absolute, the ultimate reality. This is how you can go about working efficiently in your profession, or education, or parenthood, or any role that you find yourselves in. With this method, selflessness and detached action become effortless, and you can go about life without losing sight of the truth. This subtle thought is expressed in the most famous verse of the Isha Upanishad, said to embody the entire essence of all of religious philosophy: 'All this—whatsoever moves on the earth—should be covered by the Lord. Protect your Self through that detachment.'[1] The words 'protect your Self' are especially significant because if you stay anchored in the Self, you will protect yourself from getting trapped in the endless cycles of action and reaction. You will also protect yourself from the effects of avidya, which makes you ignorant of the true nature of reality and thus entangles you in a perpetual cycle of doing and non-doing.

THE CHARIOT ANALOGY—MIND MANAGEMENT

The second method is embedded in a famous analogy from the Katha Upanishad. It describes a deep yet, at the same time, more widely applicable method which, with a fine understanding, can be applied to every moment of life. It contains within it the entire science of mind management. The Upanishad takes the example of the most common vehicle of ancient times—a horse-drawn chariot:

> Know the individual self as the master of the chariot, and the body as the chariot. Know the intellect as the charioteer, and the mind as verily the bridle. They call the organs the horses, the organs having been imagined as horses, know the objects as the roads. The discriminating people call that Self the enjoyer when It is associated with body, organs and mind.[2]

Two terms need explaining. When the word 'enjoyer' is used, it does not refer to enjoyment in the usual meaning of the word. Rather, it means 'experiencer' or 'witness'. In this sense, the witness consciousness experiences everything when associated with the mind and body. The word 'intellect' refers to the reasoning aspect of the mind, the logical faculty that helps you discriminate between the real and the unreal.

The explicit imagery of this analogy contains the secret of taking charge of your mind. An uncontrolled mind loses the power of discrimination and since the organs follow the mind, it leads to the organs making bad choices and indulging in undesirable action, just like 'vicious horses' become unruly, and lead to devastation. Conversely, if the mind is in control, the organs can be controlled through intelligent discrimination. The organs here refer not just to the physical body but also to the senses and the faculties of the mind.

If you can apply this discrimination at every point in your life, you will only be making healthier choices and steering your chariot to happiness. You, the real Self, are the master of the chariot, the latter being your body. Your intellect, the charioteer, is the key player here. It will take you to happier pastures if you allow it to make better choices. The intellect will control the horses, your mental and physical organs, using the mind as the reins or bridle. 'The objects' refers to the entire world of perception—everything physical or subtle that you can perceive. Anything that you can recognize as different from yourself is an object. The object is being referred to as a road, which means it is the path on which you can start moving.

If at this point an objection arises in your mind that you cannot control your senses, the Upanishad gives you a reassurance: 'The sense-objects are higher than the senses, and the mind is higher than the sense-objects; but the intellect is higher than the mind, and the Great Soul is higher than the intellect.'[3] In other words, do not underestimate your intellect. It can release you from suffering and bad choices, if you allow it to steer your life. It can help you differentiate between the right course of action and what your senses tempt you with. Your mind is a seat of emotions, which again can cause you to make wrong choices. Let your intellect control your mind to discern between the real and the unreal.

EXERCISES

These exercises too will not be limited to just one activity. It is for you to practise these whenever the occasion arises in life. To begin with, attempt these at least once after reading this chapter. You can write down your thoughts after practising the visualizations.

When you face any negative emotion that can cause you suffering, such as fear, anger, hatred or jealousy, or you feel like a victim of circumstances such as sickness or hurt, give yourself a few minutes to sit down and think. There are two methods you can follow here. You may choose one, depending on your spiritual or practical preference, or you may use both.

Method 1

Imagine yourself as the owner of a car, the car being your body. The engine of the car is your mind where all the emotions are located. Ahead of you is a fork in the road on which you are parked. One road is that on which secondary emotions are lined up. These emotions seem tempting because they seem to be spontaneous reactions to the sadness you are facing—revenge, depression, feeling of worthlessness, victimhood, extreme fear, self-doubt, and the like. You may have observed that whenever we are faced with sadness of any kind—failure, disease, not getting what we want—the first instinct is to rush headlong into negative thought patterns. These are bullish emotions and like the phantoms of fiction, if you drive down this dark road, these ghouls will enter the engine of your car, in this case, and stealthily enter your mind.

The other road in front of you is lined with calmer mental states like fortitude, understanding, patience, hope, gratitude, and the discernment between the real and the unreal. For most of us, these are not our primary reactions when we react to sadness or failure. Yet, that alternative road is always available. Since it requires more effort to move on that path, the negative emotions get the better of us most of the time.

You can see the fork in the road in front of you. You have to move the car now. If you put the car in self-drive mode, its engine will certainly take you to the first road which is lined with suffering. The reason? It is the shorter path, and less effort is required for you to manage your mind in this case. It is literally a self-driving licence that you give to the mind.

Now imagine you ask your intellect to get into the driver's seat. Ask it to make an informed choice. It will drive you to the peaceful road, because your intelligence can differentiate between what is worth it and what is wasteful. When you consciously put your intellect or your intelligent discernment in the driver's seat, it will make a choice that will lead you to peace.

Whenever you face disappointment or sadness, remind yourself to always put your intellect in the driver's seat. Refuse your mind when it asks you to let it move in self-drive mode. Tell your mind that you are in charge, and that you will decide where to take yourself. When faced with such a situation, imagine your intellect in the driver's seat and write down in detail how you will make the choice that will lead you to peace.

_____

_____

Method 2

This method is more suitable for those with a religious inclination. Sit quietly. Close your eyes after reading through the requirements of this exercise. Visualize the image or silhouette or the concept of God that you have in your mind. Hold the image steady in your mind for a few seconds. Now, see that presence of God gently expanding beyond its form, slowly filling the space around you, also covering you, then covering everything beyond your surroundings. It continues to expand till it covers the entire earth, but it does not stop expanding there. It keeps on spreading to cover the entire universe, as far as you can visualize.

That presence becomes everything. Hold that visualization steady in your mind. Everything has been enveloped by God. See it in your mind.

Mentally, while staying in that visualization, recall

the troubles that you are feeling. Think about whatever is making you sad. Try to locate where that sad feeling lies in the unlimited expanse of the Supreme. If you can think of yourself or your sadness as a tiny dot, look at all the other unlimited tiny dots that lie *in* the existence of God. These are all kinds of dots, happy as well as sad, painful as well as cheerful. What is the significance of this particular fading dot? It lies in God just like everything else.

If you are feeling negative emotions towards another person, see them as another speck on the fabric of this universe. That little mark too lies within the expanse of God. How then can you hate it? Everything is covered by God, so how can you love one thing and hate another?

Let the dot of your negative emotion fade away in the glory of God. As the troublesome dot fades and merges back into the unlimited expanse of God, breathe free and rest easy in the knowledge that any dot that arises in that unlimited presence will only stay for some time and then disappear. You, however, will still remain wrapped in that blissful presence.

18

CONCLUSION

ABSORBING THE KNOWLEDGE

Life is a continuous flow of all kinds of situations, happy and sad. So is the flow of our emotions perpetually changing. Even when you have had a peek into the deepest secrets of existence, your emotions will continue to rise in reaction to the difficulties of life. You may have learnt about your true blissful, limitless reality while progressing through this workbook, but you might still feel sad, angry, frustrated or disappointed, or grapple with the many challenging thoughts that are a part of being human.

However, at this point in the workbook, you have an unparalleled advantage, and that will make all the difference between how you faced suffering earlier and how you will deal with it now. You have undertaken a journey into the depths of your being. You have become familiar with that secret which the daily humdrum of life keeps hidden from us. Thus, what you have gained is nothing less than a superpower.

However, unless you practise using this superpower, it will slowly disappear. We evolve continuously, without a pause. You witness endless changes in your mind as you go through life. To use this superpower, you have to invoke it whenever the occasion arises. Slowly, it will become a habit if you internalize the ideas that you have been introduced to. This is where the exercises in this workbook will be of constant help to you.

HELP THAT IS ALWAYS AROUND

As mentioned earlier, this workbook is not a one-time read. It has been created to be a lifelong companion. The exercises are like a mirror that will help you see yourself. That is why you can revisit the workbook as many times as you want. You need not go through the entire book each time. You can go back to the sections where you can find the solutions to your problems. Each time you come back and answer the questions, you will be surprised to discover something new about yourself. This is why the exercises in this workbook can guide you on your journey towards lasting bliss.

There are several ways in which you can keep deriving benefits from this book. For some time, you can work only on the exercises on a regular basis, till the meaning settles down in your mind. Or, you may make a list of questions that you found most beneficial and keep them in a handy journal or diary. If you need help answering those questions, you can go to the relevant parts of the book and read through. During your first read, there will be certain exercises that you will want to return to and repeat. Mark them or copy them and work on them as it suits you.

Most of these practices are meant to stay in your mind as you go through your routine life, so it is not necessary to sit down and focus on the exercises, though you may feel inclined to do so. You can keep the requirements in mind and do these any time, anywhere—while commuting, cooking or taking a shower. The purpose of these practices is to help you stay in touch with your inner, tranquil reality, till it becomes effortless. If you practise, you will soon discover that you are helping yourself stay calmer and happier, no matter how troublesome the situation.

BLISS—THE SUBTLE SYMPHONY OF THE COSMOS

Nivritte sarvadukhanam[1] or the knowledge of the true Self removes all sorrows. That is the promise of Vedanta, and that is what we are striving towards. When you have the vision of the entirety of the cosmos—the secret of all secrets hidden inside of you—pain and suffering seem like frozen dew drops on leaves. They will melt away.

Just because there are problems does not mean that you have to be burdened with their weight. When you know the difference between the transitory and the permanent, the real and the unreal, you will hear the sublime notes of the grand symphony of the cosmos. You will hear the truth of your soul that never was and never will be affected by pain or suffering.

Then you will know that in order to hear the music of the universe, you only have to listen carefully. What seems unreachable is within reach. You need the right vision to see it, and the will to hear it. And then, like Tennyson's 'Ulysses', you can reach that which seems unreachable.

> To follow knowledge like a sinking star,
> Beyond the utmost bound of human thought.[2]

The journey begins with realizing that you need to remove the barrier of your ego that keeps the truth hidden from you, like a curtain veiling the splendour. What lies behind the curtain is magnificent. That is your reality, that is the Absolute Truth. It is the state where all dualities dissolve. Pain and pleasure, good and evil, love and hate, waking and dreaming, all dissolve into one reality. 'Having meditated on the Self, as bodiless in the midst of bodies, as permanent in the midst of the impermanent, and as great and pervasive, the wise person does not grieve.'[3]

As your vision becomes clearer, you will see that reality is nothing other than yourself. It is in you that everything arises and everything dissolves. Where, then, is the choice between pain and pleasure, happiness and misery? We might not be able to answer the why of existence, but we can certainly hear the whispers of the cosmos—the grand symphony of contrasting experiences that plays on while we remain forever tranquil and blissful.

ACKNOWLEDGEMENTS

Any book is a result of a lifetime of influence, observation and learning. Hence, I do not know where to begin to acknowledge all that the universe has brought together to make this book happen. This is a feeble attempt to express my gratitude.

First of all, my sincere thanks to my editor, Dibakar Ghosh, for believing in the concept and for his invaluable support right from the ideation to the beautiful execution of this book.

Many thanks to the entire team of Rupa Publications for putting it all together to bring this book out to the world.

My thanks to Ananya Sharma for the elegant cover design that beautifully visualizes the core of the book.

My sincere gratitude to Dr Payal Kumar, for her belief in me, and for being the catalyst for the beginning of my publishing journey.

The acknowledgement cannot be whole without mentioning my parents, Romesh Dutt and Madhurima, who believed in me much more than I did, and to whom I owe more than I can mention.

Thanks to Amit, Ananya and Anvesha for facilitating my journey in seen and unseen ways, and for being honest critics as well as my biggest support. Thanks to Sulbha for her unwavering support in all circumstances.

Thanks are overdue to my professors and teachers who foresaw me writing even when I was running away from it.

My everlasting gratitude to Peter Whitbread for making me believe in my talent and for prophesizing during my student days: 'I just know that one day I shall see the name Abha Sharma on a bookshelf, and I say that to very few of my students.'

A special thanks to Dr Bhupender Kumar Som, chance discussions with whom were added motivation for realizing lived spirituality.

It goes without saying that I am grateful to the numerous teachers and sources of knowledge that have been available in the form of books, videos, teachings and conversations.

It would be unfair to not mention the biggest teachers of life—sadness, grief, pain and transience—the ones that expedited the quest for answers.

My gratitude is also due to the numerous people who put their faith in me and let me into their sacred journey of pain and suffering.

Lastly, my reverential, eternal gratitude to the One that appears as many and makes all of this possible.

NOTES

Preface

1. Shakespeare, William, *The Merchant of Venice*, Act V, Scene 1, *Fifteen Poets*, Oxford at the Clarendon Press, Great Britain, 1951.
2. Greene, Brian, *Until the End of Time*, Penguin Books, 2021, p. xi.
3. Shelley, Percy Bysshe, 'Ozymandias', *Poetry Foundation*, https://tinyurl.com/3emmhzpy. Accessed on 16 December 2024.

Chapter 1: Why Most Self-Help Books Do Not Help

1. 'The Song of the Sannyâsin', *Sri Ramakrishna and Swami Vivekananda*, https://tinyurl.com/ysxwayr4. Accessed on 12 December 2024.
2. Menon, Y. Keshava, *The Mind of Adi Shankaracharya*, Jaico Publishing House, New Delhi, 1976, Reprint 1996, p. 54

Chapter 2: Let's Face It

1. 'Pain', *National Institute of Neurological Disorders and Stroke*, https://tinyurl.com/2w9kbmf9. Accessed on 12 December 2024.
2. Sagan, Carl, *Cosmos: The Story of Cosmic Evolution, Science and Civilization,* Hachette India, 1981, Reprint 2023, p. 362.
3. Barua, Arati, 'Schopenhauer's Philosophy of Will and Sankara's Advaita Vedanta', *Proceedings of the Xxii World Congress of Philosophy*, Vol. 8, 2008, pp. 23–29, https://tinyurl.com/2fteu8uh. Accessed on 18 July 2025.

Chapter 3: Pain Is Real

1. Tseng, Julie, and Jordan Poppenk, 'Brain Meta-State Transitions Demarcate Thoughts across Task Contexts Exposing the Mental

Noise of Trait Neuroticism', *Nature Communications*, Vol. 11, Article No. 3480, 2020, https://tinyurl.com/28wjztpr. Accessed on 12 December 2024.
2. Regalado, Antonio, 'Elon Musk Wants More Bandwidth between People and Machines. Do We Need It?', *MIT Technology Review*, 29 September 2023, https://tinyurl.com/448sz3x4. Accessed on 12 December 2024.
3. Gambhirananda, Swami (trans.), *Taittiriya Upanishad*, III.vi.1, in *Eight Upanishads*, Vol. I, Advaita Ashrama Publication, Kolkata, 1995, p. 398.

Chapter 4: Separate the Pain from the Suffering

1. Overbye, Dennis, 'Stephen Hawking Dies at 76; His Mind Roamed the Cosmos', *The New York Times*, 14 March 2018, https://tinyurl.com/4zscj7h7. Accessed on 13 December 2024.
2. Brockes, Emma, 'Return of the Time Lord', *The Guardian*, 27 September 2005, https://tinyurl.com/jvescv73. Accessed on 13 December 2024.
3. Dobrijevic, Daisy, 'Stephen Hawking Biography: Theories, Books & Quotes', *Space.com*, 13 May 2023, https://tinyurl.com/4jxh7ks5. Accessed on 13 December 2024.
4. Overbye, Dennis, 'Stephen Hawking Dies at 76; His Mind Roamed the Cosmos', *The New York Times*, 14 March 2018, https://tinyurl.com/4zscj7h7. Accessed on 13 December 2024.
5. 'Professor Stephen Hawking: An Appreciation by Lord Rees', *Trinity College Cambridge*, 14 March 2018, https://tinyurl.com/55djc9yc. Accessed on 13 December 2024.
6. Ramakrishna Math & Ramakrishna Mission, Mangaluru, 'Managing Suffering - The Vedantic View: Talk by Swami Sarvapriyanandaji', *YouTube*, 14 April 2024, https://tinyurl.com/4vth9tb8. Accessed on 13 December 2024.

Chapter 5: You Are Not Your Pain

1. Lord Tennyson, Alfred, 'Ulysses', *Fifteen Poets*, Oxford at the Clarendon Press, Great Britain, 1941, p. 410.
2. Ibid.

3. Sharma, Abha, *The Making of the Greatest Jack Ma,* Rupa Publications, New Delhi, 2019, p. 12.
4. Ibid., p. 49.
5. Ibid.
6. Ibid., p. 84.
7. Virupakshananda, Swami (trans.), *Samkhya Karika of Ishvara Krsna with the Tattva Kaumudi of Sri Vacaspati Misra,* Sri Ramakrishna Math, Mylapore, Chennai, Kindle Edition, 2015, pp. 128–129; '"Bending Low with Load of Life": Meaning of Human Suffering', *Advaita Ashrama,* 1 May 2021, https://tinyurl.com/bdeak8jd. Accessed on 13 December 2024.

Chapter 6: What Are You?

1. 'Personal Development Market Size and Forecast 2025 to 2034', *Precedence Research,* https://tinyurl.com/2rb645ft. Accessed on 13 December 2023.

Chapter 7: The Path to Finding the Answers

1. Gambhirananda, Swami (trans.), *Mundaka Upanishad* I.i.3, in *Eight Upanishads,* Vol. II, Advaita Ashrama Publication, Kolkata, 1995, p. 77.
2. ———, 'Advaita Prakarana', *Mandukya Upanishad,* in *Eight Upanishads,* Vol. II, Advaita Ashrama Publication, Kolkata, 1995, p. 319.
3. ———, *Kena Upanishad,* II.4, in *Eight Upanishads,* Vol. I, Advaita Ashrama Publication, Kolkata, 1995, p. 66.
4. 'The Open Secret', *Sri Ramakrishna and Swami Vivekananda,* https://tinyurl.com/2hc3jvet. Accessed on 12 December 2024.
5. Gambhirananda, Swami (trans.), *Isha Upanishad,* Verse 5, in *Eight Upanishads,* Vol. I, Advaita Ashrama Publication, Kolkata, 1995, p. 12.
6. ———, *Katha Upanishad* I.iii.12, in *Eight Upanishads,* Vol. I, Advaita Ashrama Publication, Kolkata, 1995, p. 171.
7. Chetanananda, Swami (trans.), *Avadhuta Gita: Song of the Ever-*

Free, III. 34. Advaita Ashrama Publication, Kolkata, Publication House of Ramakrishna Mutt, 1984, Reprint 2024, p. 71.
8. Ibid., III.19. pp. 64–65.
9. Gambhirananda, Swami (trans.), *Taittiriya Upanishad*, II.viii.1–4, in *Eight Upanishads*, Vol. I, Advaita Ashrama Publication, Kolkata, 1995, pp. 367–68.
10. Madhavananda, Swami (trans.), *The Brhadaranyaka Upanishad*, Advaita Ashrama Publication, Kolkata, 2023, p. 100.

Chapter 8: The Method and the Route

1. Vimuktananda, Swami (trans.), *Sri Sankaracharya's Aparokshanubhuti*, Verse 11, Advaita Ashrama Publication, Kolkata, 1938, Reprint 2022 p. 18.
2. Gambhirananda, Swami (trans.), *Katha Upanishad* II.iii.12, in *Eight Upanishads*, Vol. I, Advaita Ashrama Publication, Kolkata, 1995, p. 225.
3. ———, 'Advaita Prakarana', *Mandukya Upanishad*, III.26, in *Eight Upanishads*, Vol. II, Advaita Ashrama Publication, Kolkata, 1995, p. 298.

Chapter 9: You Are Not the Body

1. Gambhirananda, Swami, *Kena Upanishad*, I.3, in *Eight Upanishads*, Vol. I, Advaita Ashrama Publication, Kolkata, 1995, p. 48
2. ———, *Kena Upanishad*, I.4. in *Eight Upanishads*, Vol. I, Advaita Ashrama Publication, 1995, p. 49.
3. Vimuktananda, Swami (trans.), *Sri Sankaracharya's Aparokshanubhuti*, Verse 23, Advaita Ashrama Publication, Kolkata, 1938, Reprint 2022, p. 27.
4. ———, *Sri Sankaracharya's Aparokshanubhuti*, Verse 31, Advaita Ashrama Publication, Kolkata, 1938, Reprint 2022, p. 32.

Chapter 10: You Are Not the Mind

1. Nityaswarupananda, Swami (trans.), *Ashtavakra Samhita*, I.6, Advaita Ashrama Publication, Kolkata, 1969, Reprint 2022, p. 7.
2. Dattatreya, *Avadhuta Gita: Song of the Ever-Free*, II.7, Swami

Chetanananda (trans.), Advaita Ashrama Publication, Kolkata, 1988, Reprint 2024, p. 39.
3. Sarvadevananda, Swami (trans.), *Nectar of Supreme Knowledge: Yoga Vasishtha Sarah,* 2.13, Sri Ramakrishna Math, Mylapore, Chennai, 2024, p. 82.
4. ———, *Nectar of Supreme Knowledge: Yoga Vasishtha Sarah,* 4.7, Sri Ramakrishna Math, Mylapore, Chennai, 2024, p. 161.
5. Gambhirananda, Swami (trans.), 'Advaita Prakarana', *Mandukya Upanishad,* III.46–47, in *Eight Upanishads,* Vol. II, Advaita Ashrama Publication, Kolkata, 1995, pp. 318–19.

Chapter 11: The Subtle Body

1. Gambhirananda, Swami (trans.), 'Vaitathya Prakarana', *Mandukya Upanishad,* II.4, in *Eight Upanishads,* Vol. II, Advaita Ashrama Publication, Kolkata, 1995, p. 230.
2. 'Agama Prakarana', *Mandukya Upanishad* I.10–16, in *Eight Upanishads,* Vol. II, Advaita Ashrama Publication, Kolkata, 1995, pp. 206–12.
3. Gambhirananda, Swami (trans.), 'Vaitathya Prakarana', *Mandukya Upanishad* II.11, in *Eight Upanishads,* Vol. II, Advaita Ashrama Publication, Kolkata, 1995, p. 236.

Chapter 12: You Are the Witness

1. Gambhirananda, Swami (trans.), 'Advaita Prakarana', *Mandukya Upanishad,* III.29, in *Eight Upanishads,* Vol. II, Advaita Ashrama Publication, Kolkata, 1995, p. 302.
2. ———, *Kena Upanishad,* II.3, in *Eight Upanishads,* Vol. I, Advaita Ashrama Publication, Kolkata, 1995, p. 65.
3. Ibid., I.3–4, pp. 48–49.
4. Gambhirananda, Swami (trans.), *Mandukya Upanishad,* Verse 7, in *Eight Upanishads,* Vol. II, Advaita Ashrama Publication, Kolkata, 1995, p. 200.
5. Credit for the idea: Roger Ingraham Vanoro, 'A Guided Self-Inquiry Exercise - Greg Goode', *YouTube,* 17 August 2009, https://tinyurl.com/mpd66h4p. Accessed on 16 December 2024.

Chapter 13: The Mystery of the Witness

1. Griffith, Ralph T.H. (trans.), 'HYMN CLXIV. Visvedevas.', *Rig Veda*, Book 1, at *sacred-texts.com*, https://tinyurl.com/y4ndjz6a. Accessed on 21 July 2025.
2. Vivekananda Samiti, IIT Kanpur, 'Ocean and waves parable by Swami Sarvapriyananda', *YouTube*, 6 June 2019, https://tinyurl.com/32a7mzx4. Accessed on 16 December 2024.
3. Gambhirananda, Swami (trans.), 'Advaita Prakarana', *Mandukya Upanishad*, III. 6–7, in *Eight Upanishads*, Vol. II, Advaita Ashrama Publication, Kolkata, 1995, p. 274–75.
4. Sarvadevananda, Swami (trans.), *Nectar of Supreme Knowledge: Yoga Vasishtha Sarah*, 7.13, Sri Ramakrishna Math, Mylapore, Chennai, 2024, pp. 235–36.

Chapter 14: The Enigma Called Maya

1. Sharma, Abha, *Vediquant: Vedantic Truth in Quantum Science*, Rupa Publications, New Delhi, 2023, pp. 10–11.
2. Gambhirananda, Swami (trans.), *Taittiriya Upanishad*, II.i.1, in *Eight Upanishads*, Vol. I, Advaita Ashrama Publication, Kolkata, 1995, p. 304.
3. ———, *Aitareya Upanishad*, in *Eight Upanishads*, Vol. II, Advaita Ashrama Publication, Kolkata, 1995, p. 66.
4. Lokeswarananda, Swami (trans.), *Chandogya Upanishad*, Ramakrishna Math, 1998.
5. Gambhirananda, Swami (trans.), 'Agama Prakarana,' *Mandukya Upanishad*, Verse 2, in *Eight Upanishads*, Vol. II, Advaita Ashrama Publication, Kolkata, 1995, p. 175.
6. ———, 'Vaitathya Prakarana', *Mandukya Upanishad*, II.12, in *Eight Upanishads*, Vol. II, Advaita Ashrama Publication, Kolkata, 1995, p. 237.
7. Sarvadevananda, Swami (trans.), *Nectar of Supreme Knowledge: Yoga Vasishtha Sarah*, 2.11, Sri Ramakrishna Math Mylapore, Chennai, 2024, p. 79.
8. Ibid., 2.16, p. 71.
9. Gambhirananda, Swami (trans.), 'Alatashanti Prakarana', *Mandukya Upanishad*, IV.78, in *Eight Upanishads*, Vol. II,

Advaita Ashrama Publication, Kolkata, 1995, p. 383.
10. '02 Yugavani: Incarnation', *The Vedanta Kesari*, 2019, https://tinyurl.com/3wahr7ak. Accessed on 28 July 2025.
11. Experiencing Bliss, 'The Princess of Kashi | Swami Sarvapriyananda | Mandukya Karika- "No Mind" | VedantaNY', *YouTube*, 27 June 2008, https://tinyurl.com/5fyhmtht. Accessed on 16 December 2024.
12. Gambhirananda, Swami (trans.), 'Vaitathya Prakarana', *Mandukya Upanishad*, II.32, in *Eight Upanishads*, Vol. II, Advaita Ashrama Publication, Kolkata, 1995, p. 251.
13. Nityaswarupananda, Swami (trans.), *Ashtavakra Samhita*, VII.2–3, Advaita Ashrama Publication, Kolkata, 1969, Reprint 2022, p. 54.

Chapter 15: The Realization—the End of All Suffering

1. Gambhirananda, Swami (trans.), *Isha Upanishad*, Verse 7, in *Eight Upanishads*, Vol. I, Advaita Ashrama Publication, Kolkata, 1995, p. 14.
2. Dattatreya, *Avadhuta Gita: Song of the Ever-Free*, III.19, Swami Chetanananda (trans.), Advaita Ashrama Publication, Kolkata, 1988, Reprint 2024, pp. 64–65.
3. Gambhirananda, Swami (trans.), *Taittiriya Upanishad*, II.iv.1, in *Eight Upanishads*, Vol. I, Advaita Ashrama Publication, Kolkata, 1995, p. 334.
4. ———, *Katha Upanishad*, I.iii.15, in *Eight Upanishads*, Vol. I, Advaita Ashrama Publication, Kolkata, 1995, p. 176.
5. Ibid., II.ii.11, p. 206.
6. Sarvadevananda, Swami (trans.), *Nectar of Supreme Knowledge: Yoga Vasishtha Sarah*, 5.2, Sri Ramakrishna Math, Mylapore, Chennai, 2024, p. 188.

Chapter 16: A Danger and A Warning

1. Nityaswarupananda, Swami (trans.), *Ashtavakra Samhita*, XIX.1, Advaita Ashrama Publication, Kolkata, 1969, Reprint 2022, p. 184.
2. ———, *Ashtavakra Samhita*, XVIII.20, Advaita Ashrama Publication, Kolkata, 1969, Reprint 2022, p. 139.

3. Sarvadevananda, Swami (trans.), *Nectar of Supreme Knowledge: Yoga Vasishtha Sarah*, 7.1–7.2, Sri Ramakrishna Math, Mylapore, Chennai, 2024, pp. 222–23.
4. Gambhirananda, Swami (trans.), *Bhagavad Gita with the Commentary of Sankaracharya*, 3.4, Advaita Ashrama Publication, Kolkata, 2018, Reprint 2021, p. 122.
5. Ibid., 3.7, p. 125.
6. Ibid., 4.18, p. 162.
7. Ibid., 4.20, p. 169.
8. Nityaswarupananda, Swami (trans.), *Ashtavakra Samhita*, IV.1, Advaita Ashrama Publication, Kolkata, 1969, Reprint 2022, p. 43.

Chapter 17: The 'How' Question

1. Gambhirananda, Swami (trans.), *Isha Upanishad*, Verse 1, in *Eight Upanishads*, Vol. I, Advaita Ashrama Publication, Kolkata, 1995, p. 4.
2. ———, *Katha Upanishad*, I.iii.3–4, in *Eight Upanishads*, Vol. I, Advaita Ashrama Publication, Kolkata, 1995, pp. 163–64.
3. Ibid., I.ii.10, p. 168.

Chapter 18: Conclusion

1. Gambhirananda, Swami (trans.), 'Agama Prakarana', *Mandukya Karika*, I.10, *Mandukya Upanishad*, in *Eight Upanishads*, Vol. II, Advaita Ashrama Publication, Kolkata, p. 206.
2. Lord Tennyson, Alfred, 'Ulysses', *Fifteen Poets*, Oxford at the Clarendon Press, Great Britain, 1941, p. 410.
3. Gambhirananda, Swami (trans.), *Katha Upanishad*, I.ii.22, in *Eight Upanishads*, Vol. II, Advaita Ashrama Publication, p. 156.

SUGGESTED READING

Chapter 1: Why Most Self-Help Books Do Not Help

1. Sharma, Abha, *Vediquant: Vedantic Truth in Quantum Science*, Rupa Publications, New Delhi, 2023.

Chapter 8: The Method and the Route

The four-fold qualifications have been elaborated in Vedantic texts such as:
1. Vimuktananda, Swami (trans.), *Sri Sankaracharya's Aparokshanubhuti*, Advaita Ashrama Publication, Kolkata, 1938, Reprint 2022, pp. 13–18.
2. Madhavananda, Swami (trans.), *Sri Sankaracharya's Vivekacudamani*, Advaita Ashrama Publication, Kolkata, 2009, Reprint 2023, pp. 11–15.
3. Nikhilananda, Swami (trans.), *Vedanta-Sara of Sadananda*, Advaita Ashrama Publication, Kolkata, 2014, Reprint 2023, pp. 22–27.

Chapter 9: You Are Not the Body

1. Vimuktananda, Swami (trans.), *Sri Sankaracharya's Aparokshanubhuti*, Verse 23, Advaita Ashrama Publication, Kolkata, 1938, Reprint 2022, pp. 20–36.
2. Sarvadevananda, Swami (trans.), Nectar of Supreme Knowledge: Yoga Vasishtha Sarah, Sri Ramakrishna Math, Mylapore, Chennai, 2024, pp. 231–40.

Chapter 10: You Are Not the Mind

1. Vimuktananda, Swami (trans.), *Sri Sankaracharya's Aparokshanubhuti*, Advaita Ashrama Publication, Kolkata, 1938, Reprint 2022, pp. 37–41.
2. Gambhirananda, Swami (trans.), *Kena Upanishad*, in *Eight Upanishads*, Vol. I, Advaita Ashrama Publication, Kolkata, 1995, pp. 40–47.

Chapter 11: The Subtle Body

1. For further reading on the five sheaths: Gambhirananda, Swami (trans.), *Taittiriya Upanishad*, Chapters II–V, in *Eight Upanishads*, Vol. I, Advaita Ashrama Publication, Kolkata, 1995, pp. 323–342.
2. For further reading on the three states: Gambhirananda, Swami (trans.), 'Agama Prakarana' and 'Advaita Prakarana', *Mandukya Karika*, in *Eight Upanishads*, Vol. II, Advaita Ashrama Publication, Kolkata, 1995, pp. 175–307.
3. For further reading on the gold example: Nityaswarupananda, Swami (trans.), *Ashtavakra Samhita*, Advaita Ashrama Publication, Kolkata, 1969, Reprint 2022, p. 101.

Chapter 13: The Mystery of the Witness

1. Nityaswarupananda, Swami (trans.), *Ashtavakra Samhita*, Advaita Ashrama Publication, Kolkata, 1969, Reprint 2022.

Chapter 14: The Enigma Called Maya

1. Sharma, Abha, V*ediquant: Vedantic Truth in Quantum Science*, Rupa Publications, New Delhi, 2023.

Chapter 15: The Realization—the End of All Suffering

1. Sharma, Abha, *Vediquant: Vedantic Truth in Quantum Science*, Rupa Publications, New Delhi, 2023.

BIBLIOGRAPHY

'02 Yugavani: Incarnation', *The Vedanta Kesari*, 2019, https://tinyurl.com/3wahr7ak. Accessed on 28 July 2025.

'"Bending Low with Load of Life": Meaning of Human Suffering', *Advaita Ashrama*, https://tinyurl.com/bdeak8jd. Accessed on 14 December 2024.

Ashokananda, Swami, *Spiritual Practice: Its Conditions and Preliminaries*, Advaita Ashrama Kolkata, 2008, Reprint 2023.

———, *Spiritualizing Everyday Life*, Advaita Ashrama Publication, Kolkata, 1992, Reprint 2023.

Barua, Arati, 'Schopenhauer's Philosophy of Will and Sankara's Advaita Vedanta', *Proceedings of the Xxii World Congress of Philosophy*, Vol. 8, 2008, pp. 23–29, https://tinyurl.com/2fteu8uh. Accessed on 18 July 2025.

Brockes, Emma, 'Return of the Time Lord', *The Guardian*, 27 September 2005, https://tinyurl.com/jvescv73. Accessed on 13 December 2024.

Brodov, V., *Indian Philosophy in Modern Times*, Progress Publishers, Moscow, 1984.

Budhananda, Swami, *How to Build Character*, Advaita Ashrama Publication, Kolkata, 2022, Reprint 2023.

———, *The Mind and Its Control*, Advaita Ashrama Publication, Kolkata, 1971, Reprint 2023.

Chatterjee, Satischandra, and Dhirendramohan Datta, *An Introduction to Indian Philosophy*, Rupa Publications, New Delhi, 2012, Reprint 2023.

Chetanananda, Swami (trans.), *Avadhuta Gita: Song of the Ever-Free*, Advaita Ashrama, Kolkata, Publication House of Ramakrishna Mutt,1984, Reprint 2024.

Dattatreya, *Avadhuta Gita: Song of the Ever-Free*, Swami Chetanananda (trans.), Advaita Ashrama Publication, Kolkata, 1988, Reprint 2024.

Dobrijevic, Daisy, 'Stephen Hawking Biography: Theories, Books & Quotes', *Space.com*, https://tinyurl.com/4jxh7ks5. Accessed on 13 December 2024.

Experiencing Bliss, 'The Princess of Kashi | Swami Sarvapriyananda | Mandukya Karika- "No Mind" | VedantaNY', *YouTube*, 27 June 2008, https://tinyurl.com/5fyhmtht. Accessed on 16 December 2024.

Feynman, P. Richard, *Surely You're Joking Mr. Feynman*, Vintage Books, 1992.

Fifteen Poets, Oxford at the Clarendon Press, Great Britain, 1941.

Gambhirananda, Swami (trans.), *Bhagavad Gita with the Commentary of Sankaracharya*, Advaita Ashrama Publication, Kolkata, 2018, Reprint 2021.

———, *Eight Upanishads*, Vol. I, Advaita Ashrama Publication, Kolkata, 1995.

———, *Eight Upanishads*, Vol. II, Advaita Ashrama Publication, Kolkata, 1995.

Greene, Brian, *The Elegant Universe*, Vintage Books, 2000.

———, *Until the End of Time*, Penguin Books, 2021.

Hawking, Stephen, *The Theory of Everything*, Jaico Publishing House, Delhi, 2006, Reprint 2009.

———, *A Brief History of Time*, Bantam Books, 1995.

Lokeswarananda, Swami (trans.), *Chandogya Upanishad*, Ramakrishna Math, 1998.

Madhavananda, Swami (trans.), *Sri Sankaracharya's Vivekacudamani*, Advaita Ashrama Publication, Kolkata, 2009, Reprint 2023.

———, *The Brihadaranyaka Upanishad with the Commentary of Sankaracharya*, Advaita Ashrama Publication, Kolkata, 1934, Reprint 2023.

Menon, Y. Keshava, *The Mind of Adi Shankaracharya*, Jaico Publishing House, New Delhi, 1976, Reprint 1996.

Muller, Max, and T.H. Griffith, *Holy Vedas*, Grapevine India Publishers Pvt. Ltd., New Delhi, 2019.

Nikhilananda, Swami (trans.), *Drg Drsya Viveka*, Advaita Ashrama Publication, Kolkata, 1932, Reprint Nov 2021.

———, *Vedanta-Sara of Sadananda*, Advaita Ashrama Publication, Kolkata, 2014, Reprint 2023.

———, *Vivekananda: A Biography*, Advaita Ashrama Publication, Kolkata, 1964, Reprint 2023.

Nityasthananda, Swami, *The Psychological Aspects of Spiritual Life*, Advaita Ashrama Publication, Kolkata, 2019, Reprint 2024.

Nityaswarupananda, Swami (trans.), *Ashtavakra Samhita*, Advaita Ashram Publication, Kolkata, 1969, Reprint 2022.

Overbye, Dennis, 'Stephen Hawking Dies at 76; His Mind Roamed the Cosmos', *The New York Times*, 14 March 2018, https://tinyurl.com/4zscj7h7. Accessed on 13 December 2024.

'Pain', *National Institute of Neurological Disorders and Stroke*, https://tinyurl.com/2w9kbmf9. Accessed on 12 December 2024.

Paramananda, Swami, *Self Mastery*, Advaita Ashrama Publication, Kolkata, 1980, Reprint 2023.

——— (trans.), *The Upanishads*, Prakash Books India Pvt Ltd., New Delhi, 2019.

'Personal Development Market Size and Forecast 2025 to 2034', *Precedence Research*, https://tinyurl.com/2rb645ft. Accessed on 13 December 2023.

Prabhupada, Swami, and A.C. Bhaktivedanta, *Bhagavad Gita As It Is*, The Bhaktivedanta Book Trust, 1986.

Premeshananda, Swami, *Self Development*, Advaita Ashrama Publication, Kolkata, 2011, Reprint 2023.

'Professor Stephen Hawking: An Appreciation by Lord Rees', *Trinity College Cambridge*, 14 March 2018, https://tinyurl.com/55djc9yc. Accessed on 13 December 2024.

Ramakrishna Math & Ramakrishna Mission Mangaluru, 'Managing Suffering - The Vedantic View: Talk by Swami Sarvapriyanandaji', *YouTube*, 14 April 2024, https://tinyurl.com/4vth9tb8. Accessed on 13 December 2024.

Ranganathananda, Swami, *Spiritual Life of the Householder*, Advaita Ashrama Publication, Kolkata, 1999, Reprint 2023.

———, *The Approach to Truth in Vedanta*, Advaita Ashrama Publication, Kolkata, 1999, Reprint 2016.

Regalado, Antonio, 'Elon Musk Wants More Bandwidth between People and Machines. Do We Need It?', MIT Technology Review, 29 September 2023, https://tinyurl.com/448sz3x4. Accessed on 12 December 2024.

Roger Ingraham Vanoro, 'A Guided Self-Inquiry Exercise - Greg Goode', *YouTube*, 17 August, 2009, https://tinyurl.com/mpd66h4p. Accessed on 16 December 2024.

Sagan, Carl, *Cosmos: The Story of Cosmic Evolution, Science and Civilization*, Abacus, London, 1981, Reprint 2023.

Sarvadevananda, Swami (trans.), *Nectar of Supreme Knowledge: Yoga Vasishtha Sarah*, Sri Ramakrishna Math, Mylapore, Chennai, 2024.

Sharma, Abha, *The Making of the Greatest Jack Ma*, Rupa Publications, New Delhi, 2019.

———, *Vediquant: Vedantic Truth in Quantum Science*, Rupa Publications, New Delhi, 2023.

Shelley, Percy Bysshe, 'Ozymandias', *Poetry Foundation*, https://tinyurl.com/3emmhzpy. Accessed on 16 December 2024.

Sri Ramana Maharshi *Who am I? The Teachings of Sri Ramana Maharishi*, Sanage Publishing House, 2021.

'The Song of the Sannyâsin', *Sri Ramakrishna and Swami Vivekananda*, https://tinyurl.com/ysxwayr4. Accessed on 12 December 2024.

'The Open Secret', *Sri Ramakrishna and Swami Vivekananda*, https://tinyurl.com/2hc3jvet. Accessed on 12 December 2024.

Tseng, Julie, and Jordan Poppenk, 'Brain Meta-State Transitions Demarcate Thoughts across Task Contexts Exposing the Mental Noise of Trait Neuroticism', *Nature Communications*, Vol. 11, Article No. 3480, 2020, https://tinyurl.com/28wjztpr. Accessed on 12 December 2024.

Vivekananda Samiti, IIT Kanpur, 'Ocean and waves parable by Swami Sarvapriyananda', *YouTube*, 6 June 2019, https://tinyurl.

com/32a7mzx4. Accessed on 16 December 2024.

Vimuktananda, Swami (trans.), *Sri Sankaracharya's Aparokshanubhuti*, Advaita Ashram Publication, Kolkata, 1938, Reprint 2022.

Vireshwarananda, Swami, *Brahma Sutras According to Sri Sankara*, Advaita Ashrama Publication, Kolkata, 1936, Reprint 2021.

Virupakshananda, Swami (trans.), *Samkhya Karika of Ishvara Krsna with the Tattva Kaumudi of Sri Vacaspati Misra*, Sri Ramakrishna Math, Mylapore, Chennai, Kindle Edition, 2015.

Vivekananda, Swami, *Meditation and Its Methods*, Compiled by Swami Chetanananda, Advaita Ashrama Publication, Kolkata, 1980, Reprint 2023.

———, *Personality Development*, Advaita Ashrama Publication, Kolkata, 1999, Reprint 2023.

———, *Practical Vedanta*, Advaita Ashrama Publication, Kolkata 1896, Reprint 2023.

———, *Thoughts on the Gita*, Advaita Ashrama Publication, Kolkata, 2013, Reprint 2023.